ZCMI

AMERICA'S FIRST
DEPARTMENT STORE

MARTHA SONNTAG BRADLEY

All photographs courtesy of ZCMI and the Utah Historical Society.

Cover photograph by Jon Hall.

© 1991 ZCMI

ISBN 0-87579-482-3

Printed in the United States of America

10   9   8   7   6   5   4   3   2   1

CONTENTS

ACKNOWLEDGMENTS v

INTRODUCTION. 1

UNITY THROUGH COOPERATION 8

COOPERATION, 1878–1896 28

FORMATIVE, 1896–1930 55

MODERNIZATION, 1930–1960 85

EXPANSION, 1962–1986 113

INTO THE FUTURE, 1986–1991 160

APPENDIX A, DIVIDENDS ON ZCMI STOCK. . . .169

APPENDIX B, ZCMI OFFICERS. 173

APPENDIX C, HISTORIC QUOTATIONS. 189

INDEX 197

ACKNOWLEDGMENTS

FOR MANY OF THE PEOPLE who have worked at ZCMI over the years, the company is not just a business but a family. To those who have shared with me their impressions of that "family" I am grateful.

Rarely, in writing a history of this scope, is it possible to be able to interview so many of the major players. I am indebted to the presidents of ZCMI, Harold Bennett, Oakley Evans, Joseph Anderson, Lowell Durham Jr., and Richard Madsen, who have so generously provided their insights and shared their memories and their time. These are great men.

I am also indebted to Marjorie Beard, executive secretary to the president for so many years, for her invaluable work in preserving the company's history. Because of her diligence the record is rich indeed. I thank her for her efforts as well as for sharing her understanding of the company's story. Keith Saunders, Bill Coles, and Lana Pasternak provided as well their expertise, insight, and encouragement in all stages of the project. Finally, I am grateful to Nancy Mortensen for her constant support and good friendship.

INTRODUCTION

THE TROLLEY SCREECHED TO A STOP as the driver called out, "This stop: ZCMI." A mother and her daughter quickly stepped out of the streetcar before the doors slammed shut like the jaws of an enormous beast. As if by reflex, the pair looked up at the store's formidable facade and saw "Zion's Cooperative Mercantile Institution" stretch long before them. The child squeezed her mother's hand more tightly, thinking the sign surely must touch the sky.

Dodging between two delivery wagons parked in front of the store's arcade, the girl paused to pet the powerful head of the workhorse, hesitating before she ventured into the crowd of people that pushed their way through the store's front doors.

What a commanding structure! Salt Lake City's finest department store put forth a fitting face to the public with its central pedimented section, cast-iron Corinthian columns,

1

and broad sash. Despite her reluctance, the young girl could hardly wait to go inside to a world of glitter and charm matched only by the circus.

P.T. Barnum, himself a former merchandiser, once remarked that the great department store was much like a circus. Both had bright lights and a razzle-dazzle approach to marketing; both presented a plethora of colors, textures, and shapes designed to entice the eye and please the customer. Certainly ZCMI fit the mark. As one of the first retail institutions in Salt Lake City to be outfitted with its own electrical plant, it was soon filled with glittering lights that made the store's interior sparkle with wonder long into the evening hours. The store was famous for its "Festival of Lights" display just two years after the electric light bulb was first introduced. The company was often a trendsetter, leading the way with newfangled inventions such as hydraulic elevators or, in 1946, the first escalator in the Western United States.

ZCMI was one of the first stores in the West to use women as salesclerks. (In fact, some local cooperatives were managed entirely by women.) It was the first department store to start a clothing factory, the first in Salt Lake City to have delivery wagons, and, in 1920, the first to boast a motorized fleet.

ZCMI was pegged "America's First Department Store" in 1933 by author Joseph Kane in his book *Famous First Facts*.[1] Although there are at least five other contenders for this title, including Wanamaker's, Macy's, and Marshall Field, ZCMI's claim is particularly convincing. Paris had the very first department stores in the 1850s when such companies as "Au Bon Marche," "Au Printemps," and "Les Grands Magasins du Louvre" sold goods as varied as those of an international bazaar. Treasures of the world from the most mundane to

ZCMI, America's first department store.

the most exotic were available to anyone who entered their doors. This same organizational structure was soon found after 1868 in as unlikely a place as Salt Lake City, Utah, at Zion's Cooperative Mercantile Institution. ZCMI was from the very first a department store. Its unique organization, wherein several individual merchants pooled their resources and retained management of their separate areas, established a "departmental" structure from its beginning in 1868. On December 1, 1870, as soon as there were laws to allow it, ZCMI was incorporated, marking a second "first" when it became the first department store in America to become a corporation.

From the beginning ZCMI offered excitement that paralleled the best of the circus, but it was also something more. In many important ways this company was at the heart of the community. ZCMI was unique not only because it was, as one little girl put it, "Heavenly Father's department store," but because for many years it played a central and decisive role in the economy of territorial Utah. It persists as a key to any discussion of merchandising in the West. The enduring perception of the connection between ZCMI and its mentor church helped to plant its hold on the community with roots that ran both wide and deep.

But perhaps the most striking fact about ZCMI's history is that it could easily be used as a mirror of Utah's economy at large. One could not make that generalization about any other single business entity or organization in the state's history. Because of the company's perpetuity, its unique connection to the people, and its particular relationship to the dominant regional religion, The Church of Jesus Christ of Latter-day Saints, it makes a truly intriguing study.

When business was good at ZCMI, business was good in general. A graph of ZCMI's sales, or one of cash and stock dividends over time, could function as a monitor of the economic health of the community. This was not because it had an overbearing monopoly on the market (although it occasionally did), but because of the particular interconnectedness of its function in the community.

ZCMI was after all a business, but it was definitely a business with a difference. The company was never an organism unto itself, nor was it ever just a store. From its inception the company had a uniquely symbiotic relationship with the Mormon church. Like the marsupial that crawls out of the protective pouch of its mother, ZCMI grew from a notion about religion and its place in society to become something of its own. The history of ZCMI is inextricably intertwined with that of the Church.

This story falls naturally into four rather distinct time periods that correspond with developmental stages:

1. Organization, 1868–1895. This was a time of actual ecclesiastical control, promotion, and expansion. ZCMI was

4

the symbol and absolute center of cooperation and self-sufficiency for the Church.

2. Formative, 1895–1930. During this stage professional commercialized services, a significantly more stratified organization, and increased distance between Church and store leadership were achieved. The Church maintained "virtual" control over stock through stock ownership of prominent members rather than Church ownership.

3. Modernization and bureaucratization, 1930–1960. During this time ZCMI met the world on the world's own terms, competing for business with upbeat advertising, marketing, and promotion techniques. At the same time the company struggled to maintain its identity as its traditional relationship with the Church was redefined. ZCMI moved to a new place alongside the central ecclesiastical organization.

4. Expansion, 1960–1986. The addition of seven branch stores enlarged sales and the market ZCMI serviced. The Church increased its "actual" influence through ownership of 51 percent of the company's stock.

Because more of ZCMI's history runs through the years of the twentieth century than the nineteenth, comparing the store today with that of Brigham Young's day is like judging apples against oranges. But there are five basic issues that will be studied in each time period to trace policy and perception over time: (1) organization policy and structure, (2) management theory and practice, (3) employment policies, (4) public policies toward markets, charities, and the community, and (5) entrepreneurial policies.

But the story of ZCMI is also the story of people. Perhaps even more interesting than the way these policies and programs were woven together was how people fit into the overall design. The story of the "People's Store" is only as interesting as its people.

ZCMI president Harold H. Bennett was fond of telling a story about a buyer in the lingerie department, a Miss Lillian Parkinson. As was traditional, when Miss Parkinson reached the age of retirement the company honored her with a party to recognize her many years of service to the store. Mr. Bennett told her that she could bring anyone she wanted to her retirement party. She answered, "I would like to bring my mother." This surprised Bennett because Miss Parkinson was, after all, retiring because of her advanced age.

After the dinner and a number of speeches President Bennett turned to Miss Parkinson's mother and said, "Wouldn't you like to say a word?" Her mother's sweet, pale face lit up as she said, "Of course, I was afraid you weren't going to ask me."

The elderly woman leaned on her daughter's shoulder and pulled herself to her feet, carefully found her way to the podium, placed her hands on both sides of the wood, and began in a quiet whisper of a voice to speak.

"When I was only a slip of a girl my father ran a sawmill. He used to take me up in the canyon to admire the trees and to help him choose the best. One day when I was with him I heard a noise, the whirling of a saw in the trees. He took my hand and led me up to where two great piles of boards were raised.

"I asked him, 'Why do you put them in two piles? Why don't you just put them in one?'

"And he answered, 'Let me show you.'

"He showed me one pile and said that a certain board had knotholes. He pointed to another that had a crack running from the top to the end. But then he took me to the other pile and said, 'These boards are going into the building of ZCMI and every one of them must be straight and true and solid and every one must be sound.' "

At this point this beautiful elderly woman, remembering the awe this idea had aroused in her as a young girl, leaned over to Mr. Bennett and said: "Young man, you have a great responsibility. I hope you have the same respect and sense of responsibility for this institution that my father had."[2]

I have come to understand what she meant.

NOTES

1. Joseph Nathan Kane, *Famous First Facts* (New York: H.W. Wilson, 1933).

2. Interview with Harold H. Bennett by Martha S. Bradley, June 12, 1988, Salt Lake City, Utah.

UNITY THROUGH COOPERATION

THE TEN MEN KNELT IN THE MORNING sunlight that filtered through the window of the Eagle Emporium's third-story office. Brigham Young, the Mormon prophet and president of the new Zion's Cooperative Mercantile Institution, led the group in a "very impressive prayer dedicating to the Lord every particle of the building from the foundation to the roof with all its contents."[1]

Concluding his prayer, President Young rose to his feet and asked that he be the store's first customer. At 9:45 he led the board of directors, which included business and Church leaders George Q. Cannon, William Jennings, Henry W. Lawrence, Daniel H. Wells, Hiram B. Clawson, William Clayton, H. W. Naisbett, Joseph Woodmansee, and Wilford Woodruff, down three flights of stairs to the entrance. Pausing, perhaps considering the great significance of the moment, President Young stepped forward, dramatically pushed open the two heavy front doors, and proclaimed to the world that Zion's Cooperative Mercantile Institution was open for business. The store's first bill of sale was in fact for one thousand dollars' worth of goods purchased for the large family of Brigham Young.

The stage for the drama played at the doors of ZCMI on March 1, 1869, had been set earlier, in the conflict between Utah Mormons and the outsiders they derisively called "Gentiles." Even as the pioneer settlers of the Salt Lake Valley built their first homes and surveyed, marked, and leveled the streets that stretched long and straight across the valley, Brigham Young looked with dread toward the end of the geographic isolation of his people. At the same time, he accepted the inevitability of the coming of the railroad and prepared to control the change it would evoke on the territory of Utah. Ironically, as territorial governor he had helped open the door to expansion in both 1852 and 1854 by signing two transcontinental railroad bills. To Brigham Young and other leaders of the LDS Church, the railroad and the increased contact that it brought with national markets and the world outside presented a most serious threat to the cohesiveness and solidarity of the Saints. Because he anticipated trouble, confusion, and the inevitable cultural and social diversity that accompanied the railroad, Brigham Young planned what amounted to a frontal attack.

Brigham's dream of a cooperative mercantile system was one of many protective policies designed to unify the economic lives of the Saints. In addition, by the 1880s the Church had organized and promoted cooperatives, banks, mills, and factories to harbor the economic independence and self-sufficiency of the group.

The breach between Gentile merchants and the Mormon church intensified during the Utah War of the 1850s. Many Mormons believed that the dissatisfied non-Mormon population had planted in the minds of governmental agents that idea for an invasion by Federal troops on Utah territory. By the 1860s Brigham was calling loudly for some sort of action to temper the power of the merchants, who he thought pandered after the patronage of Church members and were becoming rich in the process.

Mormons were not the only important clients of merchants whose stores lined the city's main streets. In 1860 Salt Lake City was much like a typical dusty frontier town. The center of business life was Main Street, a crazy quilt of gaily painted wood storefronts, sturdy and pretentious brick buildings, and shacks already rotting and falling apart from neglect. The unpaved street itself, when not muddy or glazed with puddles, was dusty and misery to pedestrians. Spring water flooded the gutters framing the roads, and these were often clogged with trash or debris. In 1860 Salt Lake City was an important commercial hub of the West. Much like Independence or St. Louis, it served as a supply station for mining camps, immigrant trains, and the many soldiers stationed in camps like Utah's Fort Douglas.

The Mormons benefited from the traffic in goods afforded by such mercantile institutions as Walker's or Auerbach Brothers. Cash was scarce in territorial Utah, so farmers traded their homegrown and handmade goods for "state's goods." The cycle was completed when this same produce was sold to soldiers or immigrants for the cash that allowed merchants to ship in more goods. Because finished specialty

10

items were scarce, merchants charged exorbitant prices to Saints and soldiers alike. For example, in 1866 sugar sold for an unprecedented $1.00 a pound and was frequently unavailable altogether.

When President Young saw control over the financial life of his beloved community slipping through his fingers, he responded directly and succinctly in a verbal attack. In the October 1865 general conference of The Church of Jesus Christ of Latter-day Saints, the podium of the domed Tabernacle was the platform where Young declared war upon the Gentiles. He urged Mormon men of business to seize control of the market and enter into trade.

> Cease to buy from them the gewgaws and frivolous things they bring here to sell to us for our money and means—means that we should have to bring the poor here, to build our temples, and our towers, ornament our public grounds, and buildings, and to beautify our cities. For as merchandising has been generally conducted here, instead of having our means to perform these public works, it has been borne away by our enemies by the million.[2]

"Buy goods, set up stores, let our own oxen haul our freight," he continued. "This is right; it is politically right, socially and morally right, and it is right in every sense of the word for us to sustain ourselves."[3]

In combination, the discontent of the Saints at the exorbitant prices and profits of the Gentile merchants, his own personal obsession with territorial self-sufficiency, and the shadow cast by the impending railroad all strengthened Brigham Young's resolve to direct his people carefully into a full-fledged boycott against Gentile firms. Those affected by the boycott saw it as a final effort to oust outsiders once and for all. The opposition voice heard in the *Union Vedette* decried this apparent misuse of ecclesiastical power.

> Their noxiousness [the sermons'] consists mainly in the fact that they are calculated and designed to stir up the bitterness of classism and cause the people to regard all not of their peculiar faith as direct enemies of the community. They tend to keep alive a feeling of intense antagonism, resulting in personal and class vindictiveness, which every good citizen should seek to allay rather than excite.[4]

Reaction was immediate and direct. The next day, December 20, 1866, twenty-three non-Mormon firms threw in the towel and unilaterally sold out, planning to leave the territory. Their offers to sell out to the Church were declined.

After years of pressure and antagonism between Church and Gentile business leaders, Brigham Young could not resist flaunting the power and threat of the unified action of the Saints. On Sunday, December 22, 1866, two days after the largest number of firms had sold out, he spoke before a full house in the Tabernacle. His Christmas message included a taunting criticism of this "class of men who are here to pick the pockets of the Latter-day Saints." The message of unity, of self-sufficiency, of strength through cooperative effort, would identify and eventually become the banner of the co-operative movement for the next thirty years. To emphasize his point he said:

> I say, from merchants, lawyers, editors, farmers, mechanics, and all individuals who will give succor to such a class of men withdraw your support. If he is a merchant, pass by his store or place of business; serve the mechanic the same; and let every enemy of the people become satisfied that they cannot look to us for support while they, at the same time, are seeking with all their might to bring about our destruction. . . . You have no deal or communication with men who would destroy you.[5]

Within four days two Gentile firms, Firman and Munson of Nephi and J.H. McGarth of Salt Lake City, closed entirely.

Those businesses that did survive did not depend on the Mormons for their business.

The notion of cooperation was always an important part of Mormonism. Its applicability to the business sector was suggested as early as 1860 when Captain W.H. Hooper, John Sharp, Edwin D. Woolley, and Daniel H. Wells, among others, presented to Brigham Young the idea for a wholesale merchants association. The association, they proposed, would ideally benefit the entire community by creating fair price standards. Edwin D. Woolley argued that "it was time something was done to stop the bleeding of the people in regard to means." He pointed out that "there was a prejudice existing against any 'Mormon' who embarked in the business of merchandising, but there was no prejudice existing against any person who did not belong to us, no matter how much they impose upon the people and when trouble came upon us would pack up their goods and immense fortunes they had made and leave us to bear the burden."[6]

President Young agreed with the basic idea of cooperative business but he doubted that the people were ready to support it. "Why don't we instead," he proposed, "encourage home manufacturing, the community at large would benefit from the growth and support of home production."[7] When Brigham Young was finally prompted to reverse his policy of noninvolvement in stock in trade, he urged Mormons to enter the world of merchandising, thereby "ceasing to pad the pockets of those who sought the destruction of the Church." Cooperation became a hot topic of debate in conference addresses and newspaper editorials. In 1865 Albert Carrington, the editor of the *Deseret Weekly News*, was perhaps the most ardent and vocal proponent of cooperative business yet. Apostle George Q. Cannon, prominent Church and business leader, waged an editorial campaign promoting cooperation in every aspect of business. The time was right, the place unsurpassed in the history of the world, the people of Utah "can harmoniously cooperate as no other people can." Cannon saw cooperation as the great leveler, the one guarantee that capital would not be concentrated in the hands of an elite few.[8]

The dialogue surrounding cooperation accelerated during Brigham Young's boycott on Gentile merchants, which was extended in 1868 to include all "outsiders" rather than just the enemies of the people. In October conference of 1868 the Church president cautiously introduced the subject of co-operative buying, asking the Saints: "Are we of one heart and mind on this subject?" And then in the event that not all were yet convinced he added, "My feelings are that every man and woman who will not obey this counsel shall be severed from the Church." After Brigham told the people the strength of his feelings on the subject he called for a vote, "and let all who feel as I do lift up his right hand." Not surprisingly, the vote was unanimous.[9]

Brigham Young was not the only Church leader standing on the bandwagon for cooperation. Speaker after speaker at that important October conference addressed the virtues of cooperative effort, of unity in temporal affairs, and of home manufacturing. Immediately following the conference the Mormon newspapers joined in the campaign, publishing reviews of the Rochdale system of cooperation in England and its applicability to Utah communities. Flowery editorials stressed that the material oneness of the Saints would be strengthened by an exclusive commercial policy and coop-eration in business.

The boycott, the propaganda campaign, the careful intro-

14

duction of the subject of cooperation, and finally, the effort by the General Authorities to solidify broad-based support were all part of Brigham Young's plan to meet the economic challenges that he anticipated would accompany the railroad. It was a study in patience that in the leaders' way of thinking was nothing short of self-preservation. "It is our duty, we owe it to our God, to our religion, to our families and to posterity, to take measures to preserve that peace which God has so signally blessed us with up to the present. And it would be suicidal in us to contribute of our means to sustain those who are branded with our open enemies."[10]

October 1868 seemed to be the right time. Spurred by the emotion of the conference, a group of business leaders from across the territory met the following Monday morning at Salt Lake City's Social Hall. They unitedly supported a resolution to establish a cooperative wholesale store, and scheduled a series of meetings to introduce the subject to their local areas.

These men, like the imposing Abraham O. Smoot of Provo, Utah, were powerful ecclesiastical and financial leaders in their communities. They would be persuasive representatives of the Church's plan for cooperation. Apostles Wilford Woodruff and George Q. Cannon, among others, dedicated themselves to convincing the people to throw their support to the Church's store, known almost from the first as the "People's Store."

Local meetings held in churches and schools in rural communities throughout the territory were the scenes of discussion about the proposal where subscriptions for membership in the venture were sold. The small investor could buy even a single share for five dollars and be a part of the cooperative enterprise. Many paid for shares with eggs, bushels of tomatoes, or other produce. Subscriptions were then processed through the Salt Lake City office of William Hooper.

ZCMI was conceived as a great leveler, an institution capitalized by the people. In fact, men of great capital were discouraged from putting all their resources in this one pot. Before a full house at the Tabernacle, Brigham Young called for the investment of even the poorest member of the Church: "But I say to you bishops, do not let these men take five thousand, or one thousand, but call on the brethren and sisters who are poor and tell them to put in their five dollars or their twenty-five, and let those who have capital stand back and give the poor the advantage of this quick trading."[11]

Enthusiasm ran so high during that first week that within a few days, on October 15, the proposed wholesale mercantile house became a reality, formally organized and funded. This gathering of many of the most prominent Church and business leaders took place in Salt Lake's impressive new City Hall.

Local merchant Horace S. Eldredge called the meeting to order and was elected temporary chair, with William Clayton acting as secretary. William Hooper stood and announced that the purpose of the meeting was to consider the "propriety" of the idea, and to identify which merchants were willing to sell out their own businesses to join in the venture.

They talked about their concerns and about their dreams for the success of the project. Predictably, Brigham Young had much to contribute; George A. Smith, George Q. Cannon, Horace Eldredge, and others had a sympathetic audience for their arguments. The day was quickly spent and the group adjourned satisfied that the work would go forth.

Friday morning at ten o'clock the group reconvened with all who had subscribed to the store. Brigham Young personally and as the representative of the Church subscribed to $25,000 worth of stock, or 49.5 percent of the entire amount. The three largest stockholders, Brigham Young, William H. Hooper, and William Jennings, subscribed to $35,000, or 69.03 percent of the total $50,000 sold that day. The eight largest subscriptions represented 78.89 percent of the total investments. The other thirty-nine men subscribed to only 21.11 percent of the total. The price of a single share was kept low enough to allow every member of the Church the opportunity to join the association. The Church retained control of the company through stock ownership of its prominent members.

The second order of business was the election of officers. Brigham Young was unanimously elected president, with William H. Hooper, vice president; William Clayton, secretary; and David O. Calder, treasurer. The first board of directors similarly combined Church and business leaders: George A. Smith, George Q. Cannon, Horace S. Eldredge, Henry W. Lawrence, and William Jennings.[12] A committee was appointed to draft a constitution and bylaws.

After each man in the room made financial commitment to the cooperative store, Brigham Young reminded his associates of one of the original purposes of the association: price controls. "In regard to this cooperative institution it is our duty to bring goods here and sell them as low as they can possibly be sold and that the profits be divided with the people at large."[13]

Prices at the "People's Store" would not only be lower than those charged by Gentiles, but they would be uniform throughout member branches. At the Friday meeting a committee was appointed to establish a fair price scale that responded to actual values.

Founders and Officers of ZCMI in 1868. Center, Brigham Young; clockwise from top, George A. Smith, William Jennings, William Hooper, Henry W. Lawrence, Horace S. Eldredge, David O. Calder, William Clayton.

The board of directors of the new Zion's Cooperative Mercantile Institution met for the first time on October 24, 1868, to vote on the proposed constitution and bylaws. These documents told much of the unique nature and design of the organization.

In 1868, when ZCMI was officially organized, there was no statute law providing for business incorporation. It was not until two years later that ZCMI was incorporated for a period of twenty-five years under the new territorial law. The term of incorporation was renewable and limited to the twenty-five-year period but, like much in LDS doctrine and theology, the covenant binding the association was "perpetual." The notion of perpetuity was of central importance in terms of religion and social organization among the Mormons. It bound the Saints together in cooperative effort for eternity.

In the 1860s and 1870s the line between what was the Mormon church and what was ZCMI had not yet been drawn. The Church was in business; business was the Church. Through such organizations as ZCMI, the Utah Central Railroad, and Zion's Savings Association, the Church promoted the economic growth and development of the territory.

The bill of incorporation and constitution articulated the complicated mixing of religious and business motivations that backed the company. Section 20 of the constitution described the ideal character of prospective employees: "No person or persons shall be eligible for membership, except they be of good moral character and have paid their tithing according to the rules of the Church of Jesus Christ of Latter-day Saints."[14]

On October 24, 1868, the constitution and bylaws were approved, calling for an authorized capitalization of $3,000,000, consisting of 30,000 shares valued at $100 each.

The constitution provided ZCMI with its first logo—a symbol to the world of the unity of the Mormon people identifying stores joined in the association. The first such emblem was hoisted up to the top of Eldredge and Clawson's on November 13, 1868. "Holiness to the Lord" arched across the top of the sign over the familiar symbol of the "all-seeing eye." Underneath, the words "Zion's Cooperative Mercantile Institution" properly identified the building as a member store. The seal clearly symbolized the mission of the store, which was to protect the Saints from the encroaching power of the Gentiles.

As each ZCMI sign appeared, the line between insiders and outsiders was clearly drawn. The sign, designed by Midgley and Evans, was an official symbol of loyalty, a stamp of approval of Church leaders. Even those Mormon firms that chose not to associate were ostracized because of their refusal to unite. Although many merchants rallied to the cause, support for the parent store was less than universal.

ZCMI was for several months organized but essentially inoperative. At the same time co-ops were successfully functioning throughout the territory in rural communities such as Brigham City, pulling potential business from Salt Lake City. The Provo Cooperative Institution's formidable success and independent buying policy threatened the parent institution most directly. By February 1869 Brigham Young was sufficiently alarmed to solicit the renewed support of local merchants to insure that Salt Lake City would be the headquarters of the cooperative network.

William Jennings was the first Salt Lake merchant to put his entire stock into the pot, representing a $75,000 investment in ZCMI. At the February 15 board meeting Saddler and Teasdale offered their store's goods, subject to a guarantee of employment. Horace S. Eldredge and Hiram B. Clawson added their inventories the same day. Once these

The ZCMI logo readily identified member stores.

four powerful firms had joined together, a number of others—including David Day and Co., Woodmansee Brothers, and Bowman and Company—followed suit, increasing both the number and diversity of products to be sold.

This positive joining of forces provided the momentum needed to finally open the store. Just three days after Jennings threw in his support the *Deseret Weekly News* announced that the wholesale store would soon be opening, offering goods

Stores all along the street show their connection to ZCMI.

at low prices and favorable terms.[15] The next day a letter from ZCMI secretary William Clayton appeared in the *News*, announcing the opening two weeks later of the new Zion's Cooperative Mercantile Institution. After several months of deliberation, when the merchants finally moved they moved quickly.

During the following weeks the board formed policies about employment, payment, and price schedules. Uniform prices were fundamental to the concept of a parent wholesale store and its branches. President Young set the guide: "That we should know the retail prices of every settlement, and when a person comes to the parent store they should be charged the same price as their own store charges."[16] The small farmer and the person buying in bulk would be treated the same. Employees would be paid "part in cash and part in orders on the retail stores of their respective wards."[17]

ZCMI scrip and coin soon filled the pockets of farmers and merchants alike.

The feeling that all were part of a grand social experiment was fostered by the fact that before the organization of ZCMI most employees had actually been merchants themselves and had subordinated their own potential profits to the good of the group. Hiram B. Clawson, of the now-defunct firm of Eldredge and Clawson, a son-in-law of Brigham Young, was appointed general superintendent; Mormon apostle and businessman William Clayton was chief clerk; and Henry W. Naisbett became the first buyer and was sent immediately to the eastern market.

William Jennings's store, the Eagle Emporium, was on the corner of Main Street and 2nd South. It was a modern, well-lit, and prodigious front for the new business. During its first week in business ZCMI offered for sale in the Emporium building a variety of dry goods, clothing, hats and caps, boots and shoes.[18] On March 10 the company established a second branch on Main Street in the Old Constitution building; this branch carried a full line of groceries, hardware, stoves, "queensware," and farming tools. The mother store, ZCMI, was now able to satisfy the wholesale needs of the Latter-day Saints. A great revolution in the territorial economy was expected.

By 1870 one hundred and fifty local cooperatives had been established as far away as Wyoming, Idaho, Nevada, and in as unlikely a place as Deadeye, South Dakota. Wherever branch stores were found they were supplied by ZCMI Wholesale with the best local and imported goods available, at uniform prices throughout the system. Individual stores were advised not to carry large stocks but to draw instead at more frequent intervals from the wholesale department.

The Eagle Emporium became ZCMI's first retail site.

Ideally, this would increase stock turnover from one to six or seven times a year. ZCMI's wholesale departments formed the link in the chain of cooperative endeavor.

Within a month Brigham Young was convinced that ZCMI should dominate retail business as well. This would have the residual effect of freeing up men engaged in merchandise who could be better used elsewhere. "We need a retail store," Brigham asserted after much thought, "to stop so many men spending their time as retail dealers. It is an expense on the community which the people should not bear, and we want to see them employed in raising grain, sheep or cotton."[19]

For many, a Church-sponsored retail outlet was a more direct threat to their private right to property than the wholesale idea had been. Many LDS businessmen continued "in a business capacity not only without sustaining the Institution, but in direct and ungenerous rivalry thereto."[20] Brigham Young was alarmed by this apparent disloyalty and saw it as nothing short of treason. He accused the unhappy merchants, leaving no question as to his position on their actions. "This is to be deprecated because it savors of division and interferes with the idea of united importation, which alone is the guarantee for home manufacture."[21]

Home manufacture was the new catchword for the Latter-day Saint brand of the Protestant work ethic. For Brigham Young, home manufacture was a symbol of his people's willingness to put muscle into the effort to become self-sufficient. He and his fellow apostles, like Erastus Snow, preached the gospel of home industry throughout the Great Basin. "Let home manufacturing, the production of raw material from the elements, become our watchword. That employment may be furnished our sons and daughters and those who shall come unto us from distant lands."[22] *Home manufacture* furthered the goal of territorial self-sufficiency, and put the people to work. "That there be no idle among us and . . . ingenuity for the welfare and prosperity of this people for the elevation of the whole"[23] was the aim. As Church leaders exhorted and preached the twin virtues of cooperation and home manufacture they encouraged local communities to start projects: raise broom corn, sugar cane, and flax to stock ZCMI with brooms, sugar, and fine linens at a fair price, and cattle for leather to manufacture into boots and shoes. Women should raise sheep and process the wool to clothe their husbands. President Young said it was up to the women "to tell their husbands to wear home-made instead of broadcloth, I would not even wear out the cloth that has been given to me were it not that my wives and daughters want me. If they were to say, 'Brother Brigham,' wear your home-made, we like to see you in it, I would give away my broadcloth, but to please the dear creatures I wear almost anything."[24]

ZCMI was immediately successful with its shelves filled with state's goods and those manufactured at home. Signs with the all-seeing eye marked stores up and down Main Street and at least visually joined the many departments of the new store together as one. Success was pretty much guaranteed by the virtual monopoly ZCMI created almost as soon as it opened its doors. Competition had been beaten back and eliminated in many areas. The store began with the enthusiastic and broad-based support of the people, a diversified inventory, and the persuasive backing of Church leaders who waged an aggressive public-relations campaign from the pulpit to insure its continued success.

If dividends can be used as an accurate measure of the institution's profitability, ZCMI was off to a good start. A 10 percent cash dividend was issued in 1869, followed in 1870 by a 16 percent cash and 25 percent stock dividend. By September 30, 1869, a total of $289,570 had been received by ZCMI as paid-in capital by stockholders; by 1873 $782,000 had come in, and sales were $4,500,000 a year. Within four years more than half a million dollars had been declared in dividends on an original investment of $280,000. The success of the "People's Store" was enjoyed by the people.

NOTES

1. Minutes of the Board of Directors, Volume A, p. 17, October 10, 1870.

2. *Journal of Discourses*, 9:139–40, October 9, 1865.

3. Ibid.

4. *Daily Union Vedette*, December 19, 1866.

5. *Deseret Weekly News*, January 9, 1867.

6. History of Brigham Young, ms. 1860, Salt Lake City: Archives of The Church of Jesus Christ of Latter-day Saints, p. 233.

7. *Deseret Weekly News*, January 9, 1867.

8. *Deseret Weekly News*, June 17, 1868.

9. *Deseret Weekly News*, November 11, 1868.

10. *Deseret Weekly News*, October 14, 1868.

11. *Journal of Discourses*, 13:35, April 8, 1869.

12. *Deseret Weekly News*, October 16, 1868.

13. Minutes of the Board of Directors, Volume A., p. 16, October 16, 1868.

14. Constitution, Zion's Cooperative Mercantile Institution.

15. *Deseret Weekly News*, December 18, 1869.

16. Minutes of the Board of Directors, Volume A., p. 39, February 25, 1869.

17. Ibid., pp. 37–39, February 24, 1869.

18. *Deseret Weekly News*, March 2, 1869.

19. Minutes of the Board of Directors, Volume A., p. 45, March 19, 1869.

20. Ibid., p. 70, October 10, 1870.

21. Ibid.

22. *Journal of Discourses*, 19:185, June 3, 1877.

23. Ibid.

24. *Journal of Discourses*, 13:36, April 8, 1869.

Z. * C. * M. * I.

COOPERATION
1878–1896

IN THE 1870S COOPERATION SPREAD through Utah territory like mushrooms on a summer lawn. The Saints were ready to join in yet another cooperative venture and formed co-ops as easily as they had earlier joined for irrigation and colonization projects. By 1870 more than one hundred and fifty co-ops had been organized in Mormon territory, uniting the economic forces of even the most humble stockholder in the work.

Cooperation was surely the great cement that bound the people together with a powerful and effective bond. Church proponents of the cooperative principle heralded its power to unite "the interests of the capitalist, the producer, and the consumer; (it) cheapens the great staples of life; advocates the practice of justice and economy in production and exchange and secures an equitable division of profits."[1]

Church president Brigham Young watched the territory fill with Saints fresh from the field—infused with the fire of joining in with the work of the Lord. Many came from the industrial centers of England—Liverpool, Manchester, Birmingham—workers waiting for a place in the community of Saints. Discussions about the nature of this new society took place in the president's office—dreams of this "city upon a hill" that beckoned to the downtrodden and truly offered a chance for anyone willing to work.

Cooperation was nothing new to the Saints. The concept of consecration and stewardship was central to Mormon doctrine, certainly central to Joseph Smith's vision of the good society.

Brigham Young's version of cooperation had a very practical application in the 1870s. It was to be the great leveler, the equalizer that would help alleviate the poverty of those who had sacrificed everything to come to the Great Basin.

In an extraordinary document entitled an "Apostolic Circular" these ideas were promulgated throughout the Church. The Brethren read these carefully chosen words that spread the gospel of cooperation, and pondered upon their significance. Playing with the rhetoric of class conflict, Brigham expounded the virtues of the one sure solution to the labor problem: cooperation.

The circular first briefly described the long distance the American system had strayed from the "priceless legacy" of the Founding Fathers. "The wonderful growth of wealth in the hands of a comparatively few" presented the most grievous threat to the economic security of the Saints. In Utah this process had already begun, and a wealthy class was seizing control over the poor.

29

The growth of such a class was dangerous to our union; and, of all people, we stand most in need of union and to have our interests identical. Then it was that the Saints were counseled to enter into co-operation. In the absence of the necessary faith to enter upon a more perfect order revealed by the Lord unto the Church, this was felt to be the best means of drawing us together.[2]

With this sentiment and with the work of cooperation President Young was clearly in league with others who similarly worked for social change through association. The Saints marched alongside the farmers of the Grange and matched shoulders with the flannel weavers of the Rochdale pioneers in England in a grand social experiment. Such people believed in the potential of association for evoking positive change in the world and for liberating the working classes.

The Mormon cooperative mirrored most closely the Rochdale industrial cooperative in practice in England during the last half of the nineteenth century. Although there were some significant differences in the way the two systems worked, they shared similar objectives. Perhaps the most significant divergence was that the Mormon cooperative was above all the expression of a religious ideal. ZCMI was in one way unmistakably the Church's store — the "all-seeing eye" clearly and unabashedly branded it as the temporal arm of the Church. But it was also, as Brigham soon began calling it, the "People's Store." The broad-based public ownership of the local cooperatives insured that the people themselves shared in the success or failure of this united venture.

Metaphorically a parent-child relationship was often used to describe the connection between ZCMI and the Church, as well as that between ZCMI and the cooperative network. As one contemporary observed:

ZCMI, it is called the parent institution; and it ought to be the parent of all these institutions as a father and benefactor, doing all it can to promote the welfare and prosperity of the people, to protect it and sustain it by doing their business throughout that institution and act prudently, wisely, orderly, and unitedly in regard to those matters that we may be one.[3]

In 1869 the Saints had before them two successful examples of cooperation on which to base their new organizations: one in Lehi and the other in Brigham City, Utah. As owners of these newly formed co-ops, local members dictated the shape and color their stores would take.

In Brigham City, what began as a retail cooperative soon expanded to include virtually all manufacturing and merchandising interests. This model was soon repeated in isolated areas throughout the Mormon colonies and was particularly effective in those places least subject to intrusions from the outside world.

The effect of the cooperative system on the economy at large is difficult to assess because of the complicated intermixing of what was in some cases every aspect of the economic life of the community. Obviously, profits are not the only measure of the effect cooperation had on the economy. Cooperative businesses employed thousands of Saints who in turn pumped their money back into the system as consumers. During the 1870s and 1880s ZCMI's business represented an estimated one-third of the total expenditures of Utah. The company was of central importance to the economic health of the community.

It was clear that the Mormons were expected to support ZCMI. Although in the extreme case, excommunication awaited those unwilling to bow to the direction to support the company, more often a soft push in the right direction sufficed.

Often the pressure was less direct but every bit as potent. The year 1871 was a disastrous one for farming in Weston, Idaho. A spiteful drought sucked moisture from the earth, leaving miles and miles of parched, useless soil. What wheat and oats were raised were shipped and sold to freighters in the nearest trade center at Corinne, the Gentile capital of Utah. One group of Mormon farmers went into Corinne, sold their crops, and decided to buy stoves to surprise their wives. One man bought a bright brass-and-iron stove for $37.50 and with another $2.50 bought a pair of shoes. The farmers went home happy, relieved that their wives would no longer have to kneel before the hearth to cook. When their local bishop, Bishop Maughan, heard that they had bought stoves in Corinne from Gentile merchants, he threatened to cut them off from the Church. "You should have bought your stoves through ZCMI," he said, "even though the price is $50.00."

By the next Sunday the story had spread through town. One elderly woman stood up in the meeting and expressed the general sentiment, "I would never eat food cooked on a Gentile stove." After the meeting the bishop invited the farmers separately into his home so they could ask for forgiveness. "You should say you are sorry for what you have done," Bishop Maughan said, "even though you did get an awfully good deal." One man, a Welsh immigrant named John Evans, felt so much remorse that he offered to throw the stove away if he could only be forgiven.[4]

The Church continued to nurse ZCMI along during its first two decades in operation. Support on the part of Church leaders was ever present, and they provided expert advice or funds when needed.

An example of this Church support occurred in the winter of 1871-72. This winter was particularly harsh; monstrous

32

piles of snow and ice blocked the passage of even the most sturdy trains or freight wagons. Merchandise en route to ZCMI valued at $120,000 sat stalled in railroad cars long after the thirty days after invoice when payment was due. Brigham Young, as president of ZCMI and trustee-in-trust of The Church of Jesus Christ of Latter-day Saints, loaned the institution $160,000 without interest, to be used as collateral in borrowing the money to meet its notes coming due.

This curious mixture of Church and business typified the company's leadership and management during the nineteenth century. At the head of the corporation sat men whose combined ecclesiastical and economic power pulled them above the crowd. But unlike typical merchants bound by self-interest, men such as Horace Eldredge and Hiram Clawson had already subordinated their own interests for the good of the community of Saints. This brand of "public virtue" gave their work a new sense of significance in the plan of salvation.

In 1875 ZCMI's board of directors included Church president Brigham Young, apostle George Q. Cannon, and William Henry Hooper, Horace S. Eldredge, David O. Calder, Aurelia Miner, Christopher Layton, and George Reynolds — a prestigious lineup of people entrenched in power at the heart of the business life of Salt Lake City. William Hooper, for one, was a former state senator and president of the National Bank of Deseret. He gave a masterful speech in defense of polygamy before the United States Forty-first Congress on March 24, 1870. Hooper had worked as a steamboat captain on the Mississippi River before joining the Church and coming to Utah. He worked as superintendent of ZCMI from 1873 to 1875. Upon the death of Brigham Young, Hooper was elected president of ZCMI, a position he held until his death in 1881.

Like William Hooper, Horace S. Eldredge was a polyga-
mist; he had five wives and twenty children. Between May
1870 and June 1871 Eldredge presided over the European
mission while continuing to serve on the board of ZCMI.
These men, who divided their time between family, business,
and Church responsibilities, typified ZCMI's early leadership.

Besides its geographic expansion through the network of
cooperatives, ZCMI expanded in terms of physical facilities.
In April 1875 the board moved to consolidate many of ZCMI's
entities under one roof. The committee that was organized
to choose a building site purchased land from Brigham Young
for $30,000 on a ten-year loan at 12 percent. The *Deseret Weekly
News* recorded the laying of the foundation, which was one
"of the most substantial and enduring of any similar structure
in the West, and the basement is so far as we are aware,
larger than that connected with any other building in the
Territory."[5] Along the lower level, craftsmen laid warm red
brick manufactured at the Bountiful Co-operative Brick Yard
and shipped to the Temple Block by the Utah Central Railroad.

On August 3, the *News* reported:

> The ZCMI new building continues to go up rapidly. Mr. Henry
> Grow and his corps of hands have nearly finished the laying of the
> joists of the first floor, all of the timbers of which, including the huge
> supports, are of excellent Utah pine, which for strength and dura-
> bility can scarcely be excelled.
> The laying of the brick portions of the walls has been commenced,
> and they will now rise rapidly. The stonework is completed, with
> the exception of a small portion.[6]

The *News* also mentioned that reporters as far away as
Omaha, Nebraska, followed the erection of ZCMI's new
home.

ZCMI's expanded store stretched three stories high.

Eighty-one clerks, porters and salesmen are employed. . . . The second story has been reached. . . . A steam engine is used to hoist the brick and mortar. The front will be of iron. The walls are of brick. It is three stories high and has a basement besides. The building is 318 feet long by 54 feet wide, and an L will be built 50 × 100. A track will be laid from the depot to the back door so that cars can be unloaded at a trifling expense. A yard 150 feet square will be for the accommodation of customers from the country, and this space will be surrounded with sheds for stock. Everything considered, this is perhaps the most extensive mercantile establishment west of Chicago, and few houses in that city will surpass it in extent of business and dimensions of store.[7]

The facade of ZCMI's new home frontage spanned fifty-two feet down Salt Lake City's Main Street across from the Old Constitution building. Three stories and a full basement soon filled with a variety of goods for retail and wholesale customers.

Finally ZCMI had a unified center from which home-

A ZCMI delivery wagon stands ready.

manufactured and state's goods could radiate out to branch stores, and where shelves were lined with bright and tempting products. Local newspapers advertised the variety of home-grown and produced goods available at ZCMI: fruit in season, rainbow-hued fabrics and yarns, tools for every purpose, whips, saddles, harnesses, and castings. "There are articles of use, and articles suggestive; articles simple, and articles recherche; articles for amusement and articles requiring intellect for their appreciation."[8] The trunks and stoves available at ZCMI sparkled with brass trim and markings and represented the finest craftsmanship. The store's team of six horses, five harnesses, five wagons, or single dray insured express delivery in any weather.

The expansion of ZCMI into Ogden was a direct response to the threat posed by Gentile merchants in Corinne. "ZCMI, at Ogden, had a mission to perform for the Mormon community. . . . Its Ogden Branch has been this resistive bulwark needed by the Mormon community."[9] The Ogden branch of ZCMI was the result of a coming together of the

The new Ogden branch of ZCMI, dedicated February 1881.

firms of Perry and Herrick, the Ogden Co-op, and the mercantile institution of ex-Mayor Farr. D.H. Perry was elected by the board as superintendent of the newly created entity. In 1880 the Ogden branch got a new home for an estimated cost of $70,000 — a handsome building described as "medieval Corinthian, with a slight indication of the Tuscan."[10] The new structure was outfitted with speaking tubes that connected each floor and office, and water and gas pipes that provided convenient service and comfortable temperatures. Employees were reminded at the dedication ceremonies held on Friday, February 4, 1881, that they were part of ZCMI and had a responsibility to act accordingly.

The idea of establishing a full-scale branch operation in Logan, Utah, was first introduced by Brigham Young in February of 1872, but it was another year before the building was ready for business.

ZCMI's expansion was carefully watched by outsiders, particularly those Gentile merchants whose business had been severely affected by Brigham Young's boycott. The distrust felt by these men filtered East to the financial institutions so important to the future of a fledgling retail company. Men like Eldredge in a January 1872 trip East carefully courted the support of banks and lending companies that could so easily make or break ZCMI's future success. These men acknowledged the hand of Providence "in averting the mischief sought to be done the Institution, from time to time by untruthful men, who, through the public press and by other means, have sought to injure its business at home and to impair its fair commercial standing."[11] Before extending credit to ZCMI, firms carefully checked for themselves the soundness of the institution's financial condition.

N.G. Dun and Company monitored ZCMI's business between 1877 and 1888. In a series of interesting telegrams and letters Dun investigators acknowledged criticisms of the institution but found much that was positive in future prospects for the company. Despite predictions that ZCMI would fall after Brigham Young's death, Dun and Company described a transition that was instead smooth, stable, and in fact prophetic of a bright and prosperous future.

These fears of collapse were perhaps not unfounded. They are reminiscent of a remark made by Ralph Waldo Emerson that an institution reflects the shadow of its leader. This was certainly true with ZCMI. This pioneer institution was truly created in the shadow of Brigham Young. His philosophy, his policy, his money directed the company's growth during its first ten years.

Upon President Young's death, notice was sent immediately to all creditors that ZCMI's business would proceed as usual: "We take the liberty of saying to you and others, that his death will in no way affect the business or management of the Institution, which continues as heretofore. Its financial condition warrants us in saying, that its obligations will be met with the same promptness which has characterized all its transactions."[12]

Brigham Young was not a passive titular company president who sat back and let others direct the action. Instead he made his mark on even the most insignificant aspect of business. J. Golden Kimball enjoyed telling how Brigham Young would walk through ZCMI, and if he saw anything that was of inferior quality, he would haul out his cane and destroy it right then rather than leave it for sale. Kimball remembered that one time when President Young walked through the housewares department he found a mirror that was "wavy." He raised his cane and smashed it into a thousand pieces, saying, "We don't sell that to anyone!"[13]

Just as President Young advised Saints on private matters in their homes, he instructed employees on appropriate behavior in the Church's stores: "The brethren of the stores must first of all cease to drink liquor. They must cease taking home bottles of liquor, cans of fruit, candies, nuts and other things, they must be just in their dealings with the people and attentive to their business."[14] Saints employed by ZCMI were required to pay tithing, and were not to run excessive credit accounts.

At a meeting held October 5, 1877, stockholders elected William H. Hooper as the new president of the company. Hooper brought to the job many years' expertise in merchandising and the support and respect of business and ecclesiastical leaders alike. He was particularly well suited to weather the strain caused by Brigham Young's death. During the transition period he paid Young's heirs the $100,000 loaned to the institution by its former president and ever-present mentor. Before a year had ended Hooper had declared a 5 1/2 percent stock dividend, set aside $65,000 to provide for real estate and bad debts, and put 5 percent of the year's profits in reserve.[15]

Hooper continued Young's policy of expansion with a new addition to the main building. This additional fifty feet of storefront increased the square footage to twelve thousand.

A second area of expansion reflected the legacy of President Young's obsession with home manufacturing and territorial self-sufficiency. When ZCMI purchased the Deseret Tanning and Manufacturing Association in April 1879, it expanded upon the base the shoe factory had already created. Along with the ZCMI clothing factory, this cooperative venture helped stock shelves of cooperatives across the Wasatch Front with locally produced and marketed goods.

Brigham Young and his counselors saw home manufacture as the key to independence from the outside world and continually counseled the people to look for new products to manufacture. George A. Smith echoed this sentiment in the Tabernacle on May 6, 1870, before a gathering of Saints:

> Why send abroad for our cloth when we have the necessary means and skill to manufacture it for ourselves? Why not let these mountains produce the fine wool? and why not let the low valleys produce the silk, flax, and all other articles that are necessary which it is possible to produce within the range of our climate, and thus secure to ourselves independence? . . . If we continue to import our hats, bonnets, boots, shoes and clothing, . . . we shall ever remain dependent upon the labor of others for many of the actual necessaries of life. If, on the other hand, we devise means to produce them from the elements by our own labor we keep our money at home, and it can be used for other and more noble purposes, and we become independent.[16]

Looking into the future, in 1870 the board of directors purchased the William Sloan boot and shoe establishment known as the Big Boot Store, located on Main Street next to Walker Brothers. Despite a promising start, the business soon failed and was closed in 1873.

Not long after, in March 1874, twenty-five shoemakers organized as "The Workingmen's Cooperative Association," donating 10 percent of their monthly earnings to the capital stock. After floundering for three years with little direction, the cooperative willingly sold out to William H. Rowe.

Before he joined the Church and immigrated to America, William H. Rowe had apprenticed and worked in the shoe and leather industry. Under his able direction the company, later known as the Deseret Tanning and Manufacturing Association, became one of the most productive and efficient manufacturing institutions in the West. Rowe instituted modern, systematic methods of construction and was in fact the pioneer of modern shoe manufacturing in Utah. He brought in skilled workers from Massachusetts to educate men selected to run the machines. They introduced modern techniques of cutting, fitting, design, and marketing, insuring that the Deseret Tanning and Manufacturing Association had the best to offer. When it was evident that Rowe had something good going at the factory, the directors of ZCMI convinced him to sell the business to ZCMI with the provision that he continue as manager. Within two years the number of employees in ZCMI's shoe factory had grown to one hundred and fifty, plus ten in the tannery. By April 1883 the productive capacity of the shoe factory had doubled. After 1883 Rowe managed the clothing factory as well.

Not all was as productive as this for ZCMI. When the decade of the 1880s began, Utah's political scene could not

Workers pose in the ZCMI shoe factory.

have been more confused. With federal marshals chasing Church leaders into hiding and relentlessly badgering them into deserting their polygamous families, government and ecclesiastical systems of authority were in disarray. Even so, the future for ZCMI seemed promising. Having proven its viability in the main for twelve years of business, the company had survived the downward spiral of prices initiated by the depression of 1873 and in fact had come out stronger where many other businesses had failed.

On October 9, 1880, the departmental organization already in place at ZCMI was streamlined. Managers for both retail and wholesale departments were appointed for the different divisions. These heads were to be held strictly accountable for both employees and products under their supervision. To increase incentive and profitability, department managers received a percentage of net profits in addition to their salaries.

Hooper served as president of ZCMI from 1877, after Brigham Young's death, until January 1881, when the prophet John Taylor was voted in as president. Hooper helped ZCMI move from behind the shadow of one man to become an effective business entity in its own right. As president of ZCMI John Taylor pulled back even farther, letting management and the board of directors take primary responsibility for policy decisions.

The Church's confrontation with the United States government absorbed Taylor's primary time and energy, forcing him and his fellow Church leaders into hiding. During the 1880s Church government was conducted in large measure from farmhouses and other secret locations outside Salt Lake City and the center of the Church. Obviously, during the years of the "underground," as this time period is usually known, the business of a company governed by a group of prominent polygamists would be affected. But how?

The threat of the proposed amendment to the Edmunds-Tucker Bill, which called for the escheatment of all Church property, caused the leaders to search for ways to legally protect Church entities. Businessman and Church apostle Heber J. Grant masterminded the transaction of 350,000 shares of ZCMI stock into a private syndicate headed by Grant to protect the Church's interests in the company. The balance of 16,400 shares were sold to private individuals. By June 28, 1886, the Church had disposed of all its holdings in ZCMI; at least for a time the Church and ZCMI were financially separate. When Edmunds-Tucker was repealed the Church started to repurchase the stock.

Before 1885 there is little indication in ZCMI's official records of the tension that marked all contact with the world outside. There is only an occasional hint of the pressure that board members felt: "Good business despite the pressure that has been brought to bear upon the people by the harsh, arbitrary and cruel enforcement of severe, despotic laws and consequent feeling of uncertainty in all financial matters, which such conditions engender it is gratifying to realize that we have done well."[17]

And they did. During a period of time in 1885 when no board meetings were officially held in Salt Lake City, President John Taylor attended no meetings at all. ZCMI experienced unprecedented expansion when all business transactions were conducted in secret locations. The main building, for instance, was again enlarged with a third addition in 1891, this time to the north. In 1887 the company built a new shoe and clothing factory behind the main store, at a cost of $53,000.

ZCMI's clothing factory was the largest west of Chicago and employed three hundred men, women, and children. Each year more than 100,000 jumpers, overalls, negligees, shirts, and pieces of underclothing were manufactured at home in Utah territory. These were proudly marketed alongside Eastern "imports."

At the time of this enormous expansion board member George Q. Cannon, who took an active role in the company, was one of the most fervently sought-after polygamists on the federal marshall's list — a fact that surely affected the company. On February 1, 1885, Cannon and John Taylor went on the underground to conduct Church business in hiding. Because of John Taylor's advanced age and the absence of counselor Joseph F. Smith in Hawaii, Gentiles generally regarded George Q. Cannon as the acting president of the

Church, dominating financial and political affairs. Despite his central position in the business of ZCMI, he attended no meetings during 1885. Cannon did venture out on January 16, 1886, to a meeting held at the main store in Salt Lake City. Tension increased as federal marshals stormed Cannon's farm three weeks later, on February 7. The next day raids on the Gardo house, the president's office, the tithing house, and the historian's office circled ZCMI's main building. On February 10 Cannon's farm was raided again. Having narrowly escaped arrest two days earlier, Cannon hoped to continue his game of hide-and-seek with the agents, hiding in the private railroad car of fellow board member John Sharp on his way to Mexico and the relative legal anonymity therein. After his eventual arrest and incarceration Cannon became very ill and appeared before the court in decrepit condition. Bail set at $25,000 for his first indictment in the charge of cohabitation was paid by Sharp. The second $10,000 was paid by Horace Eldredge, then superintendent of ZCMI. Cannon forfeited both bonds and escaped.

The polygamy question did affect business but, interestingly enough, not in the way expected. During the underground, business at ZCMI expanded greatly. Many ironically believed "business was one thing and religion another. They call it a political question and do not deal in politics. But sell goods to good parties."[18]

John Taylor had a number of forces working against his active participation with ZCMI. The unique political climate in territorial Utah, his personality and temperament, his declining health and physical condition made him a very different president from Brigham Young. President Young had an intimate, active, close identification with the work. For John Taylor ZCMI was just one of many pressing problems.

The company appeared to be ably led by professional merchants who efficiently held the reins in his absence; he more often than not left it at that. There is some indication that some board members preferred it that way, doubting his ability to maneuver delicate business transactions.

Nevertheless, President John Taylor recognized the importance of the connection between the Church and the business of ZCMI. He saw ZCMI's workers as representatives of the Church, of the gospel of Jesus Christ. The government of the company, he said, should "characterize the pure in heart." Only those whose honesty and integrity was above question should be employed. "We need honorable men," Taylor continued, "who can be trusted here or anywhere, and men who are full of fraud must be cast out, as no check system will make them honorable."[19] More often such men moved into the retail business independent of any connection with ZCMI.

ZCMI clearly had a monopoly on business in Utah territory, but because of its unique organizational structure its ultimate success was dependent on the prosperity of the people. In the same way that ZCMI put an artificial freeze on certain goods, it controlled wages. Many employees were frustrated by the fact that they could be making more money on their own—and some went so far as to quit and start their own businesses.[20] William Jennings was the most prominent defection on the management level.

The company's interests and those of the Church were inextricably linked during the 1880s. Because of this relationship Church business as well as territorial business affected ZCMI's business. "On the whole the institution is the Mormon Church and the Mormon Church is the people of

Officers and directors of ZCMI in 1881. Clockwise from top: John Taylor, Joseph F. Smith, Moses Thatcher, D. O. Calder, T. G. Webber, John Sharp, Horace S. Eldredge, George Q. Cannon. Center top, W. H. Hooper; center bottom, William Jennings.

47

Utah and the success of the institution rests more on the financial ability of its managers than on any competition."[21]

When John Taylor died in November 1887, lending houses in New York City recognized ZCMI as a solid investment, always prompt in payment of bills, with a net worth of over one million dollars. "One such house says they will buy any paper of theirs that they can find in the market. Their trade, it was said, was coveted by all."[22]

Perhaps because of the company's hard-won stability as well as the political climate, which was quickly coming to a head, Taylor's successor, Wilford Woodruff, pulled one step even farther back from Brigham Young's charismatic interventionist approach to running the business. One outside observer noted that Woodruff "takes no active part in the business, which is controlled by vice president Horace S. Eldredge [and] superintendent Thomas Webber," the latter (in the opinion of that observer) "being the brains of the institution."[23]

Almost twenty years after its organization, ZCMI was run by adept leaders whose expertise was based in experience both in and outside the Church-controlled cooperative system. The managerial structure of store superintendent, treasurer, and departmental managers functioned relatively independent of the board of directors and the president of the institution. This management structure, superimposed upon store management, posed the clearest link between ZCMI and the Church. When used as a focal point of the changing relationship between the two bodies, it illustrated the different ways ecclesiastical and financial power were exercised. ZCMI mirrored what was happening to the Church in the larger community.

Change was also expressed in the increased professionalization and secularization of the company. Management emphasized quality of services rather than loyalty to the principle of oneness. The cooperative principle had proven its effectiveness in merchandising, but the fervor with which it was preached declined as the Church faced a new century and a new effort to meet the world on its own terms.

The *ZCMI Advocate*, an in-store newsletter, paraded before stockholders and employees the religion of good business during the middle years of the 1880s. Advice ranged from methods of arranging attractive window displays to descriptions of the latest fashions, from propaganda against the possibly fatal evils of using imitation butter (oleomargarine) to the importance of stock turnover. The *Advocate*'s abrupt discontinuance in 1887 was yet another effect of the wake of Edmunds-Tucker: its editor went on the underground.

During its few first years in publication, the *ZCMI Advocate* advertised the newest fashions that enlivened the racks and shelves of ZCMI's ladies department with bright colors, exotic designs and patterns, laces, beads, and sashes. Come see the "vast varieties of seasonable goods," it enticed, "from the ugly and commonplace to the comely and aesthetic; towering crown, peaked and dented as it were, in all possible and hitherto believed impossible shapes. Surely the masculine mind is utterly oblivious as to how these crude forms will appear when bedecked with ribbons, feathers, flowers, lace and multifarious trimmings." We can exclaim "involuntarily great is the mystery of fashion and wonderful the adaptations of designing women."[24]

Fashionable accessories in league with the best offered in the East included "short walking jackets, dolmans plain and braided, and new marks, the famous Paisley shawls, single and double of style running back to Persia and times im-

Sales personnel show off a variety of goods at ZCMI.

memorial and now passed as heirlooms from mother to daughter."[25]

The *Advocate* was first published ostensibly to prove the "potency of co-operation," pass information to stockholders and employees, and support the commitment to nonimportation in favor of home manufacture.[26] But as the market was filled with a proliferation of state's goods, home manufactures became less popular, and many a female Saint passed over a home-grown-and-manufactured broom for the lighter, more trimly cut version made back East. Though the process was a gradual one, change was inevitable.

Who does not remember the thick, heavy hats of home creation, with material enough in them to divide into half a dozen? Who has forgotten when good sorghum syrup was hauled around in coal oil barrels and coal oil cans. Who has not seen the quiet dwindling of our home-made soap, if the sun or wind but looked at it for a day? . . . Brooms required a man power to wield them, and to haul a home-made trunk we needed almost a yoke of cattle. Yet praise is due to the pioneers in all these directions, many of them worked unselfishly and for the public good, they sensed the situation, the counsel always ready prompted men along the forbidding path of public duty.[27]

The voice of management was also heard through the organ of the *ZCMI Advocate*. Here was one place salesclerks learned what was expected of them on the job.

The brusque, off-hand salesman cannot be a popular one, neither can he who appears indifferent, or seems to lack animation, create for himself customers who will linger for his appearance. . . . Interest in the purchaser, that is to goods needed; recommending, suggesting, introducing with modest manner new or probably needed goods, is expected of every salesman.[28]

Not all employees (or for that matter all board members) were entirely satisfied in their work at ZCMI. The company became increasingly secularized and a more diversified economy offered profitable opportunities outside. As penalties for disloyalty became less frequent, those unwilling to bow to the power of ecclesiastical leadership chose to leave or were encouraged to find work elsewhere.

Considerable controversy surrounded the demotion and eventual departure of Septimus Sears, for one, who during the week of December 2, 1889, was dropped as both superintendent and member of the board of directors. Thomas Webber was assigned the uncomfortable task of firing this longtime associate of ZCMI. Webber's resentment rings clear in the record and was directed against John Taylor's counselor George Q. Cannon, whose "arbitrary" power he objected to most vehemently. William Rowe was another employee on the management level whose capricious rise and fall and subsequent dismissal as manager of the clothing factory reflected Church politics as much as his individual abilities. Rowe resigned in 1893 as a statement against what he saw as a "unilateral disregard of his person," soon taking another job "which entailed less work and was vastly more lucrative and one in which I felt my opportunities for doing good were much greater."[29]

Portents of the massive depression that would sweep across the country in 1893 were already felt in Utah territory as early as 1891. The scarcity of Eastern capital and exorbitant rates of interest spurred a panic far worse than that of 1873. By 1893, a year long to be remembered for its financial disasters, agricultural depression extended the effects of the diseased economy across the board. Utah in particular felt the blow of low prices for silver. The many mines that shut down completely contributed to Salt Lake City's extraordinary 1893 unemployment rate of 48 percent.

As home manufacturing faltered, cooperatives failed in communities across the territory. Local co-ops liquidated because of lack of capital and a history of injudicious credit, which in hard times haunted an already shaky financial base. Increased competition forced many businesses to close their doors.

One solution to this tightening in the economy was an early portent of twentieth-century easy-credit plans, called "approval business." Customers selected their purchases, but rather than charge them, took them home on "approval." After three days, if they were less than satisfied they could return their goods. A sales representative called on these customers with a horse-drawn carriage to pick up the goods or formalize the charge. This more-than-generous practice continued until 1915.

A great amount of barter trade continued well into the first two decades of the new century. Every Saturday morning farmers from Millcreek, Bountiful, and other outlying areas would haul in their wagons spilling over with chickens, eggs, and cheese. In return they were given "merchandise vouchers," which entitled them to purchase goods at the store. This constant source of fresh produce was a sure draw for new customers.

Saturday mornings were also known to salesclerks as "Indian days," for Saturday was the day that Indians pulled into town on the morning train. When they came into ZCMI the Indians asked for John Allred, the "calico bishop," who worked in domestics selling piece goods. Their most popular purchase was buckskin needles to use in sewing their animal skins.

ZCMI, like the rest of the community, met with hard times in the 1890s, and great stringency was needed to weather the storm. Sales dipped to a new low but soon started to rise.

By September 1893 the company had expanded to include four branch stores at Ogden, Logan, Provo, and Soda Springs, Idaho; numerous cooperatives; and two major factories. Stockholders and patrons alike called for the immediate reincorporation of the company, which had proven its viability over many years of solid business. It was a time of nostalgia with the deaths of Jennings in 1886 and Eldredge in 1888. Most of the original players were dead, but their legacy of integrity in business and a belief in the importance of their work bound them to the next generation. These new leaders looked to a bright future of increased competition and loosened control from ZCMI's Church sponsor.

Notes

1. Minutes of the Board of Directors, Volume C, p. 120, April 5.
2. Apostolic Circular, 1876.
3. Minutes of the Board of Directors, Volume D, p. 9, February 14, 1885.
4. Leonard Arrington, *Pacific Historical Review* 20(May 1951):153–55.
5. *Deseret Weekly News,* June 25, 1875.
6. *Deseret Weekly News,* August 3, 1875.
7. *Deseret Weekly News,* September 18, 1875.
8. *ZCMI Advocate,* November 8, 1885, p. 7.
9. Edward Tullidge, *History of Salt Lake City* (Salt Lake City: Star Printing Co., 1886), p. 204.
10. Ibid, p. 205.
11. Minutes of the Board of Directors, Volume B, p. 47, April 5, 1873.
12. Ibid., August 24, 1877, p. 27.
13. ZCMI History File.
14. Minutes of the Board of Directors, Volume B, p. 67, October 7, 1873.
15. Ibid., October 3, 1877, p. 263; April 5, 1878, p. 296.
16. *Journal of Discourses,* 14:12, May 6, 1870.
17. Minutes of the Board of Directors, Volume C, p. 400, March 10, 1886.
18. R.J. Dun file, March 14, 1882.
19. Minutes of the Board of Directors, Volume C, p. 88.
20. Dun, February 28, 1882.
21. Ibid.
22. Dun, March 14, 1882.
23. Dun, November 9, 1887.
24. *ZCMI Advocate,* March 15, 1886, p. 57.
25. Ibid., September 15, 1885, p. 8.
26. Ibid., November 15, 1885, p. 9.
27. Ibid., October 15, 1885, p. 9.
28. Ibid., April 15, 1885, p. 11.
29. Minutes of the Board of Directors, Volume D, p. 388, November 20, 1893.

ZCMI

FORMATIVE
1896–1930

THE YEAR 1896 MARKED FOR UTAH the end of one era and the beginning of another. After six attempts, Utah territory finally became the forty-sixth state to enter the Union. In many ways 1896 was a watershed year for Utah's political, social, and economic life. Church and business leaders were eager to throw past differences aside and cautiously look to a bright new future.

The period between 1896 and 1930 was one of great expansion in agriculture, mining, and business. But the economy tended to move two steps daringly forward and one back. In the postwar years the "perils of prosperity" would mean for Utah years of recovery from a devastating slump in business.

ZCMI's growth mirrored that of the state at large. As the

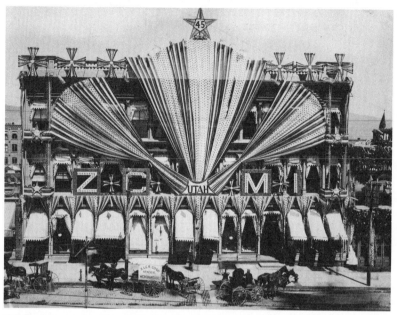

ZCMI celebrates Utah's statehood with elaborate storefront decorations.

population of Utah more than doubled between 1890 and 1920 (from 210,779 to 449,396), sales at ZCMI increased three and a half times, from $3,893,171 in 1896 to $13,207,251. Somehow ZCMI had expanded its appeal to include more than just the most faithful. The company was no longer simply the mercantile arm of a closed community, but had thrown open its doors to the business of the entire region.

The decline of ecclesiastical control and orientation at ZCMI occurred simultaneously with an increased commercialization of the company. ZCMI changed and for the first time met the world of the twentieth century on its own terms. For the new ZCMI, success was measured in net profits, not only by how well the company served the best interests of the community of Saints. Those who were affected most by the success or failure of the "People's Store" were stockholders.

Although everyone benefited from ZCMI's fair price standards and credit policies, dollars in profit now measured the relative financial health of the institution.

Changed policy also explained in part the commercialization of the company. ZCMI had traditionally paid employees partly in cash and partly in store goods or "scrip" modeled on the Church's tithing system of exchange. After the 1890s employees were paid in cash only. And a subtle change occurred in the way Church leaders promoted the store. By the last years of the nineteenth century, General Authorities no longer persuaded Saints to shop first at ZCMI through the coercive threat of excommunication or disfellowshipment. Traditional loyalties continued to connect the Latter-day Saint people to the store, but Church leaders no longer waged public relations campaigns from the pulpit for support of the "People's Store." ZCMI had to beef up its advertising budget and more aggressively and professionally parade its wares before the buying public, independent of Church channels of communication.

A new and ever-specialized variety of competing shops tried to pull business away from ZCMI with often-ridiculous price cuts and offers of scarce goods. Competition increased dramatically when the official prohibition against independent retailing was lifted. Even more than that, however, during this period the fabric of Utah society increased in complexity like the patterns of a rich brocade.

Like the floodtide of immigrants moving from rural America into cities across the nation, many Utah farmers were drawn to the excitement and promise of life in the urban centers. By 1920, 48 percent of all Utahns lived in cities. Although agriculture continued to be the mainstay of the Utah economy, business offered to many the lure of untold riches and opportunities. Fewer than 5,000 Utahns were involved in trade either as retailers or wholesalers in 1890; by 1910 that number had more than doubled, to 12,000. The streets of Salt Lake City's busy business district spoke of this expansion. A colorful, sometimes chaotic lineup of banks, retail stores, and service businesses offered a new, exciting variety of ways to satisfy one's every whim.

And ZCMI was right in the center of it all. Its imposing cast-iron facade hovered three stories over the hub of Main Street's business region. The city's new "electrified" streetcars screeched to a stop at its front doors, spilling out shoppers who for just seven cents had come from any point in downtown Salt Lake City.

One enthusiastic writer described the institution that stood at the physical heart of Utah's business community as the "balance wheel" of Utah's economy. And this was in many ways accurate. When business was good at ZCMI, business was generally good. On the other hand, the reverse was equally true. In Utah there was an unmistakable and perhaps unavoidable interdependence between agriculture, mining, and business. ZCMI's success reflected the success of the region.

Eastern bankers recognized ZCMI stock as a solid investment. In 1891, when board member and Church apostle Heber J. Grant traveled to the East to raise funds for a new bank, he certified that fact. Borrowing on the basis of ZCMI notes, Grant received unheard-of amounts at inordinately low interest rates and, more important, with very little resistance.[1]

The commercialization of ZCMI reflected that new strength and respectability. Similarly, the stratification of the business organization reflected a new level of sophistication in business techniques and services. As had always been the case, the president of the Mormon church was the titular president of the organization. He along with the board of directors held ultimate responsibility in the decision-making process.

When Lorenzo Snow became the Latter-day Saint prophet he also, on September 15, 1898, became the president of Zion's Cooperative Mercantile Institution. He enthusiastically, albeit humbly, vowed to give his best efforts. He was eighty-six years old at the time. Snow, his predecessor Wilford Woodruff, and Joseph F. Smith, who would follow him as president just three years later in 1901, were the last of the first generation of Mormon leaders. Many of the company's other leadership positions were filled by the sons and grandsons of the early stalwarts of the Church. This new group had a different agenda to fulfill, which included easing the strains that had separated the Church from the rest of the world.

Lorenzo Snow as president of the largest mercantile organization in the new state of Utah chose to take a back seat to his apostles who served on the board of directors. At the turn of the century the finances of the Church were still in disarray from the political dysfunctions of the 1880s and 1890s. Snow made a personal campaign of the concept of tithe paying and rededicated the Church to "the Lord's law of revenue." Pulling the Church out of some businesses altogether, Snow retained some minority control over others that it had promoted. Both ZCMI and the *Deseret News* could continue to serve the interests of the Church with minimal interference.

Members of the board of directors varied in their involvement and commitment to the institution. Some, like Heber J. Grant, were at the center of each major policy or legal

President Heber J. Grant maintained a close involvement with ZCMI.

decision that was made. Grant was typically the advocate of the store, meeting with banks to resolve debt conflicts or generating funds for periodic crises. His was a hands-on, intense involvement that illuminated his own personal aptitude for business. When he became president of ZCMI in 1918, it was the culmination of thirty-six years of service to the company. President Heber J. Grant knew the company inside and out. And as president he continued this tradition of involvement despite the incredible demands he felt from the Church itself, which had increased dramatically in numbers and complexity.

Other board members attended meetings and helped to form policy, but chose to direct their primary attentions elsewhere. This level of commitment and the amount of energy and attention these men gave to ZCMI depended in part on the continued dependence Church leaders had on the company for a part of their income. In an era when The Church of Jesus Christ of Latter-day Saints continued to maintain a financially independent lay ministry, General Authorities did what they could to support their families. This accounts at least in part for the large number of Church authorities who continued to sit on the board of directors despite the fact that the business of the Church and the company were moving farther and farther apart.

The board of directors was the controlling authority in the company. In 1900 the board was evenly divided between General Authorities and community business leaders. The executive committee of the board was the real arbiter of power. Of its three members, two—Heber J. Grant and George Romney—were Church apostles. The third, John R. Barnes, was a senator in the first legislature of the state of Utah and a director in ten different business institutions in Salt Lake City, including the Deseret National and Savings Bank. These three men considered a number of different projects, as simple as fixing salaries or opening new departments, or as complex and broad as plans of operation.

Until he resigned on April 17, 1919, Thomas G. Webber directed the next level of management. As superintendent (sometimes called general manager), Webber led the day-to-day activity of the store. A full-time employee of ZCMI, he focused his entire attention on the success of the company. He was the on-site head of the company; all decisions, policies, and procedures had to pass his approval before being instituted. Webber was the general supervisor over all departments.

Thomas G. Webber, general manager of ZCMI from 1888 to 1919.

Thomas G. Webber's crisp English accent and trim demeanor epitomized the new ZCMI that offered polished, professional department-store shopping equaling that of any other city in the nation. Webber was twenty-seven years old when he first came to Utah territory. After serving with the United States Army and traveling to Panama, New York City, and Washington, D.C., he felt as if he had seen the world. Webber became disillusioned with the army while serving in the Civil War and he was anxious to begin a new life in the West. He rose from the waters of baptism on February 22, 1864, feeling cleansed, purified, and dedicated to the work of the Kingdom.

That same year Webber, along with T.B.H. Stenhouse, founded the *Salt Lake Daily Telegraph*, where he worked until 1869. His life typified that of the early leaders of ZCMI: a complicated mixture of business projects and Church service. During the fifty years that Webber was employed by ZCMI he worked in a number of positions, including secretary,

secretary-treasurer, and finally superintendent, a position he held until a few months before his death at age eighty-three.

The next level of the organization was middle management. This included the managers who directed the internal affairs of their own departments. Department managers were the conduit through which instructions from the board of directors filtered down to the local level. However, operations were largely directed by their own personal initiative, and Webber seemed to allow a significant degree of autonomy in the separate departments.

During the forty-five years that Asahel H. Woodruff was with ZCMI he moved from a job as errand boy to become manager of ZCMI's wholesale dry goods department. Woodruff, like most of the company's leaders, left twice to serve missions, first in England and later as president of the Northern States Mission. Woodruff was guaranteed full pay during his mission, and was promised his same job upon his return. While Woodruff was away on buying trips or on his two missions, the affairs of the department continued on an even keel, thanks to the able management of a staff of assistant managers. One, Charles E. Erickson, first worked in the dry goods department as a salesclerk but later found it more profitable to sell on the road. Erickson was a model salesman. His fellow employees praised him for his "perseverance, his thoroughness, and his attention to detail."[2] As one of the company's team of traveling salesmen he brought ZCMI to the country, crisscrossing the state, traveling regularly from Lehi to Santaquin, Eureka, and Heber.

When Thomas G. Webber resigned as superintendent of ZCMI on May 15, 1919, it sealed the passing of the old guard. Webber, who had ably continued to lead the company well into his eighties, was of the old school of conservative preservationists who had resisted change demanded by the changed times. His replacement, John F. Bennett, was a symbol of the new generation of leaders of ZCMI who would be connected with their predecessors by traditional bonds. Many had bloodlines that stretched back to the very conception of a people's store; for others the connection was simply tradition—customary ties of loyalty to the institution. But a new generation they were—many of them college-educated professionals, bringing with them years of experience in marketing, merchandising, and advertising, much of it learned outside of ZCMI. And they were ready to apply that insight, that know-how, to the business of ZCMI. This new elite quorum of company leaders would continue to be connected to the leadership of The Church of Jesus Christ of Latter-day Saints, however indirectly.

When Webber resigned as superintendent the board of directors initiated a search for a suitable replacement. During the interim they realigned internal lines of authority and appointed John F. Bennett as vice president and chairman of the executive committee, both positions of power and prestige. This shifting and tightening of control came just two years after Heber J. Grant replaced Joseph F. Smith as president of the company. The ensuing enhanced stratification of the organization reflected the particular combination of forces and minds at work, for whom order and clear, predictable lines of authority were paramount.

In much the same way that Brigham Young had packed upper management with officers who were his own personal favorites, Heber J. Grant shuffled and laid on the table a new lineup of directors and management personnel that mirrored his own attitudes and plans for the future of ZCMI. In an unprecedented shakeup of traditional company leadership,

Grant appointed Anthon H. Lund as first vice president, replacing George Reynolds, who after thirty-five years on the board retired. Reynolds was another of the final arbiters of the hand of Brigham in the affairs of ZCMI. In the 1870s Reynolds had been President Young's personal secretary. At age eighty-nine he had little more to contribute; his primary loyalty was to the memory of what had been. Lund, on the other hand, was Grant's ally; he was equally committed to keeping ZCMI in its position of preeminence in Utah's mercantile community. Progress was the new rallying cry generated by the prosperity of the war years.

After several months of discussion and examination of the qualifications of several worthy candidates, the board failed to find any applicant for general manager whose business approach matched the goals of ZCMI's new team and the new chair of the executive committee, John F. Bennett (another of Grant's favorites). Bennett declined the general manager position but proposed instead that he become a managing director who would oversee the affairs of the institution. From that point forward, the executive committee was designated as "The Management." An unspoken underlying assumption saw this as a temporary measure until a new superintendent was found, although Bennett would serve until 1931.

From the top this arrangement looked promising, but to others it was a problem. John F. Bennett's first priority was and would continue to be his own business, Bennett Glass and Paint. After only a few months complaints began to surface. Some questioned Bennett's ability to divide his attention between many equally important commitments. Manager Claude Barnes, representing the interests of an unspecified number of stockholders, raised the issue that the

John F. Bennett, general manager of ZCMI from 1920 to 1931.

company needed to have a superintendent who could devote all his time to his duties. Graciously he acknowledged that Mr. Bennett was a capable man, but "on account of his many duties he is not able to give but a portion of his time. . . . A man should be appointed with equal capacity."[3]

John F. Bennett had never worked at ZCMI before the board appointed him managing director, but he bore the imprint of many years' work in retailing. Bennett sharpened his selling skills as a young man peddling the products of the S.R. Marks Furniture Company, Dinwoodey Furniture Company, and the Sears Glass and Paint Company. While on ZCMI's board of directors he stretched his time between the business he had founded himself, Bennett Glass and Paint, and commitments to the boards of Zion's Savings Bank, Utah State National Bank, Deseret Book Company, Home Fire Insurance, Zion's Benefit Building Society, and the Utah Oil Refining Company, among others. Like most active Mormon men he juggled two busy lives: one in business and one in the Church, where he served as a member of the Deseret Sunday School Union Board and as a member of the Church Auditing Committee.

As ZCMI's managing director, Bennett immediately sought to upgrade systems of accountability, record keeping, and accounts management. Under his direction the organization became more stratified. A high priority was to make upper management more responsive to the suggestions of the employees themselves.

Inevitably, each time an organization becomes more stratified, more complex, it involves not only greater numbers of specialists at the top but larger numbers of employees at the bottom. Even a cursory look at payroll ledgers of the period reveals not only differences in assigned jobs and responsibilities but a significant gap in wages between upper management and workers.

Fred Meyer managed the "G" Department (grocery) during 1902 for a monthly salary of $270. The salary of his assistant manager, William T. Seare, was almost two-thirds less, at $100. Each of the ten salesclerks received between $80 and $50 for his work. The one female salesclerk was paid much less than her male counterparts: $30 a month. ZCMI, as was typical of the period, paid women across the board less than men for their labor. The company was compelled on May 8, 1919, to put into effect the new eight-hour female labor restriction.[4]

Each department had a fleet of errand boys and girls who breathlessly ran messages from building to building, carted wrapped packages to the delivery dock, or did whatever type of work was required. In 1895, ZCMI's cash boys earned a total of $2,307. This included compensation for all errand boys, delivery boys, extra hands hired for bargain sales, and cash boys who worked as "gofers" throughout the store. The next year that figure doubled as girls were added to the force for the first time. Child workers were ever present at ZCMI throughout the system of factories, warehouses, and retail and wholesale stores. They provided a much-needed, inexpensive supply of unskilled labor. Many would stay with the company as adults.

For example, James Maurice Saville first worked at ZCMI in 1883 as a cash boy. By 1903 he was department manager of Chinaware. Harold E. Young periodically worked as a cash boy after school or on Saturdays in the shoe or grocery departments. In 1918 Young was the manager of ZCMI's wholesale department. George Reed worked in the drug department in the late 1880s when as a boy it "fell to his lot to make himself generally useful." After graduating from the menial duties given the average boy, Reed became a salesman "back of the counter." For a number of years he slept on the premises to take emergency calls. Occasionally, "distracted fathers would awaken him from his slumbers at all hours of the night that they might obtain paregoric for their baby with the colic, or some other cause about as serious."[5] Reed would be rewarded for his faithful service, eventually becoming a registered pharmacist.

Accounts of work conditions for child laborers in ZCMI's stores and factories varied dramatically. According to Annie Bywater, manager of ZCMI's clothing factory, girls working at ZCMI were content, productive, and efficient. "Here, happy Utah girls—with the aid of some of the most modern machinery and methods—are turning out close to 10,000 garments a month, girls and machinery constantly being added to keep pace with the increasing demand for the product."[6]

Contradicting that pleasant image another study, this one done by Hazel Youngberg in her 1907 postgraduate research, found that the internal regulation system of the overall factory failed to provide the necessary safeguards for the child employee. One small girl was given the job of snipping the end threads from a pile of overalls. Her load was placed in a dark and narrow passageway where she bent over her work struggling to see while quite efficiently wielding her scissors to put the finishing touches on the product of the factory. One observer felt the enormity of the child's plight, saying: "Those visitors who brushed past her in the passageway thought nothing of one little girl so employed, but had she been one of a hundred workers the public would have been aroused to decry in indignation an intolerable condition. But alone, or with nine-ninety comrades in misery, her injury is the same."[7]

There is no extant record of the relative ages of ZCMI's employees, but differences in wages are one indication. There was a substantial number of base-level employees whose wages were way below the average. It is also obvious in the photographic record that a significant number of ZCMI's workers were children. In one photograph of ZCMI's fifty-three shoe factory employees, thirteen were men, fifteen were boys, and twenty-five were girls between the ages of thirteen and sixteen.

As ZCMI's corporate organization changed, a variety of new programs coordinated and served the needs of all employees. The beginning years of the period were ones of laissez-faire, when the government had not yet assumed responsibility for the welfare of its private citizens. On August 16, 1897, ZCMI's employees organized a Mutual Aid Society for all workers who were in need: the company's incapacitated, pregnant, or elderly workers. In addition to aid for the sick or distressed, the Mutual Aid Society supported a number of missionaries while they served abroad. This self-sustaining fund represented the accumulated contributions of the workers themselves and a $1,000 donation from the board of directors, who readily supported the idea.

In May 1922, part of the fourth floor was remodeled into a cafeteria and ladies rest room that would be run by the Mutual Aid Society. Five hundred employees celebrated the event with an evening lunch, community singing, and lectures given by representatives of the employees themselves.

What organization was accomplished among the employees of ZCMI was like the Mutual Aid Society: informal, in-house, and welfare oriented, rather than association with a national labor union. Employees were hired on the basis of their "ability and fitness for the work required, and entirely without regard to affiliation with any union or other organization."[8] ZCMI did continue to have an unwritten set of assumptions about the moral and intellectual fiber of its workers, who were to restrain from indulging in alcohol, tobacco, or other habits scorned by Mormon society. Betting on the horse races resulted in mandatory dismissal.

The annual employee Lagoon Day was a great leveler for the company, mixing in competition the most lofty manager with the lowest delivery boy. This summer day began at dawn with an eight-mile cycle race, departmental competition in baseball games, and shooting matches. More inventive games pulled even the most hesitant into the spotlight to compete for prizes from none other than—ZCMI. The winner of the Girls' Hat and Parasol Race walked away under her parasol. For those who qualified for the Fat Man's Handicap, shoes were the prize. For the rapid few in the Hundred-Yard Dash or the Potato Paring Contest, gloves and pants were the reward. Days like this, the annual employees' ball, and other social events served as a symbol of goodwill between management and the workers.

Departmental meetings were held regularly to inform employees of changes in policy or in-house regulations. Periodically handbooks of employee rules and regulations were published by upper management and circulated throughout the store. On the evening of October 16, 1919, traveling salesmen met at Hotel Utah for an extravagant dinner and speeches by Assistant Manager Tingey, Managing Director Bennett, and Secretary-Treasurer Orlob.

In 1925, 332 employees attended the "Salesmanship and Personal Efficiency" classes at the University of Utah Extension Division. The presentation, "Ten Keys to the Purse," offered methods to improve efficiency, personal carriage, appearance, outlook on life, and determination to succeed.

This was expressive of a pervasive notion that ZCMI was indeed part of the world yet something different, something apart. The "spirit" of the institution was referred to as a given; the "People's Store" had a mission—to "save and build up rather than ruthlessly bankrupt its customers."[9] Even a lowly salesclerk at ZCMI's dry goods counter was a representative of this important work, an intermediary who effected positive influence on the life of the public.

Fourteen years after the foundation of the Mutual Aid Society, the executive committee of the board developed its own plan to provide for longtime employees of ZCMI who were about to retire. The pension plan centered on the notion of rewarding the efforts of the men and women who had worked full time at the company. At sixty-five years of age mandatory retirement held the promise of partial protection from the vicissitudes of old age. The payment scale reflected years in service and salary. A man who had worked ten years at an average salary of $80 would receive a pension of $20 a month. Such a salary drop would obviously mean a substantial drop in the standard of living, but the plan was still an important step in the direction of providing for the future of the store's employees. ZCMI had been more like a family than a business, but in these years when it became too large a family — when the commercial business aspects dominated the attentions of management and employees alike — it was necessary for the board to step in and offer the same type of service to its elderly that families did.

To some extent, ZCMI had always had a policy of helping its own. On February 19, 1903, a small twelve-year-old boy climbed to the precipitous height of a ladder and stretched to dust the boxes that sat on the top shelf of ZCMI's millinery department. He accidentally fell backward, striking his head, and soon sank into unconsciousness. After a brief examination by the company doctor, store superintendent Thomas Webber took the boy home by carriage, where he noted the family's poverty. They were short of provisions, fuel, and adequate bedding and clothing. Over the next two days the boy continued to fail, and finally he died.

Mrs. Rosina Marti had depended on her son's wages since her husband's death. She petitioned ZCMI for satisfaction for her loss to the sum of $2,000. She met with the board of directors in the institution's third-floor office with an interpreter and her attorney, Daniel B. Richards. Mrs. Marti expressed her gratitude for what the company had done to help but pointed out that in her pitiful circumstances it was not enough. She had depended on her dead son as the sole means of support for herself and her other children. "If ZCMI was not willing to pay $2,000," she said, "she would accept $1,000." The money was given to her to help her obtain a home and support "until such time as she could, with the aid of her children, make a living; on condition of full release." In times of crisis or conflict the leaders of ZCMI tried to make things right.[10]

Another important part of upgrading the professional services of the company was making the wage scale meet standards set throughout the city. The executive committee studied ZCMI's wages in relation to those of other firms and found alarming discrepancies that had, because of the high cost of living, caused bad feelings at ZCMI. Competitive firms were offering higher wages and unbelievable bonuses to lure ZCMI's loyal employees away. The committee recommended a 15 percent increase to be effective immediately.[11]

Traditionally the company attempted to remain apolitical. Frequent memos reminded employees not to discuss politics during work hours. Yet in times of national crisis ZCMI jumped forward for the national defense. During the Spanish American War young men were offered full-time wages during their period of service and a guarantee of a good job upon their return. Fully as generous an offer as for missionaries, this policy supported the war effort. On Saturday, July 19, 1899, the grand facade was gaily decorated with flags and colorful streamers that danced through the air with a warm welcome home to volunteers from the war in the Philippines.

ZCMI displays a patriotic face.

The store remained closed for the entire day to honor these patriotic young men.

A large part of ZCMI's modernization effort involved the company's physical facilities. In 1900, people walking into the lobby of ZCMI were dazzled by hundreds of electric light bulbs that played against one another, lighting a plethora of goods to please and beguile the customer. Ten acres of floor space were filled with booths, tables, and racks displaying the most up-to-date products available. A system of "speaking tubes" linked the several departments; two nickel-plated tracks and a series of basket stations followed the tops of the counters, facilitating the movement of packages to the delivery dock. Windows of the Main Street arcade stretched 200 feet, filled with the latest frilly dresses and paisley shawls. Pot-bellied stoves and children's doll buggies, trains, and whirligig toys beckoned customers inside.

Department managers spent a good deal of their time considering new ways to arrange stock to best attract the eye of shoppers. They often rearranged the interior of the store to use more efficiently the limited space. In 1901 the ready-to-wear department was expanded and moved from the third floor to the second floor. Alongside the best new millinery, underwear, and corsets, it filled two hundred feet of the second floor of the Main Street front. Exotic perfumes seeped out of the new ladies' beauty parlor and lounge. Walls that had earlier divided the separate departments were removed for a more inviting appearance of one large floor.[12] The next year a cry for a general renovation became a popular source of discussion at the store. After twenty-five years with only minor changes ZCMI was, in the opinion of many, out of date: "Much of the interior is not only out of date but very much worn. . . . The interior fillings should be so arranged as to save all the labor possible; at the same time it should offer to our friends and patrons a more attractive place to do their business in."[13]

Even more important, to those who cared, was that ZCMI's competitors were fitted in the "modern style which has rendered them attractive and has been a means of drawing trade. Our store windows are small, too high above the sidewalk, and it is impossible to attract attention."[14] As is often the case in business, competition gave the final push for change.

One way John F. Bennett modernized the company was by changing the sign that welcomed customers to the store. "Holiness to the Lord" was after 1920 reserved for Church buildings and was no longer the symbol of ZCMI.

In addition to the Main Street store ZCMI's series of buildings stretched across downtown Salt Lake City. The warehouse for the wholesale grocery department had three acres of floor space. The noise of trains pulling out of the neighboring Denver and Rio Grande depot shook the upper windows of this new structure, which had been built for $35,000 in April 1905. One block southeast of the Union Pacific depot on South Temple stood another of ZCMI's wholesale outlets—this time hardware. This allegedly fireproof building was bought earlier in the same year.

Between 1868 and 1924 ZCMI included eight separate departments: Dry Goods, Grocery, Hardware, Shoes, Chinaware, Rugs, Men's Clothing, and Meats. Each department had both retail and wholesale divisions.

The ZCMI clothing factory, located at 57 Regent Street, was for many years one of the leading manufacturing institutions of the state. The company's overalls and "all-overs" were sold from the Pacific Coast to Denver, and from Canada to Mexico. Manager Annie Bywater was trained in the factories of the English cotton industry in Lancashire. Working to capacity, the factory could put out 100 dozen pairs of overalls in a single day.

ZCMI's shoe factory was the only one in the state in 1921. Traditionally the factory had confined its work to unlined work shoes, but added machinery, lasts, patterns, and other equipment suitable for making a line of semi-fine shoes for businessmen and boys. The work of home manufacture continued to be an important part of ZCMI's business until the mid-1920s and was a recognized essential link in the economic system.

> Snappy styles such as these, made for quality and service insure an instant demand for the new lines, giving the people of this inland empire an opportunity of keeping the wheels of industry going, furnishing employment to many of our people and becoming Pay Roll Builders in very deed. The home dollar is the very best—let's keep it rolling among Utah's industries and her citizens.[15]

For a few years in the early 1930s ZCMI owned three "College Boot Stores," located in Salt Lake City, Ogden, and Logan.

ZCMI's delivery system radiated out of a sturdy brick stable located east of the main building. The metal roof of the stable and barn housed forty-two horses, wagons, carts, and a wheelbarrow used for deliveries in town. A garage was built for a cost of $20,000 on Fourth South between Fourth and Fifth West to house ZCMI's new fleet of automobiles.

When R.J. Strong first worked for the express department of ZCMI in 1918, the "garage" was a modern barn housing ninety-six head of horses. By 1921 the new automobile garage was equipped with "right-up-to-the-moment" equipment for washing, repairing, and painting the cars. Deliveries were made in Salt Lake City three times a day as far south as Ninth South, and beyond that twice daily. As many as 1,500 parcels were handled in a single day. A "large, airy, well-lighted lunch and reading room," lockers, and bathroom with six showers made work at the garage more amenable. The workers threw sociables for their "escorts and the officers of the institution" in this modern facility. "After doing full justice to a sumptuous repast, the tables were cleared away and dancing was indulged in until the approach of the 'wee small hours.' "[16]

The board of directors had been reluctant to change over to delivery by gas-powered automobiles. L.C. Snow, general manager of the Utah Auto Company, first approached them with the idea in 1906. Snow proposed that the management of ZCMI use an Oldsmobile free of charge for one month — including in this irresistible offer the driver's salary, the cost of oil and gasoline, and a daily wash and polish. It wasn't, however, until several months later that the board accepted the offer; it was several months more before the executive committee approved the purchase of an automobile for the delivery fleet.

Ideally, the board of directors functioned as a check on the power of the management. But often this complicated division of power impeded the decision making and made change difficult and time consuming.

In many ways the period between 1896 and 1925 was one of incredible expansion, but it was also a time of tightening, of concentration in terms of administration and power. The networks of cooperatives that connected the rural communities of Utah together like the tentacles of a sea monster steadily diminished in business. Most of them took a secondary position in the trade of the local areas, some even lower. The board of ZCMI resisted the idea of buying them out altogether, but sought new ways of pumping life back into the system. One member suggested organizing the group more closely by bringing them under the management of traveling superintendents who would visit stores, examine account books, revive the credit system, update stock, and in general establish a direct line from ZCMI to the sister stores. But this would have divided the resources and energies of the company in several different directions at a time when concentration and centralization of power was the pervading goal. The two ideals were contradictory impulses, and as a result the cooperative system was allowed to wither and die in most regions of the state.

The first of the branch stores to be sold was in Provo, where competition had virtually forced ZCMI out of business. After a year of fighting the inevitable, the Logan branch was sold on December 19, 1901, just months after the Rexburg, Idaho, store had been converted into a warehouse. Five years later, declining profits and increased overhead forced the sale of the Ogden branch. By 1906, then, centralization, at least in terms of physical facilities, was complete. Operating from a central location in Salt Lake City, ZCMI conducted its business from the parent store and a system of local warehouses located in Idaho and throughout Utah. This offered the advantage of direct access to a wide range of merchandise sources from which buyers could search out goods needed by farmers in isolated locations.

Buying philosophy reflected this change, moving from "What do I have to sell?" to "What does the customer want?" This sharper and more rational definition of business purpose, coupled with volume purchasing and streamlined distribution, made the first ten years of the twentieth century some of the best in the company's history.

Rapid growth demanded that drastic changes be made in the company's operating methods. These efforts mirrored the objectives of the scientific movement that was such an important part of the reform era.

A series of figures monitored business during the first decades of the twentieth century — none as important as stock turnover. Stock turnover was for many a symbol of the volume of merchandise that moved in and out of the store. One author wrote for the *ZCMI Advocate*: "Buy often, buy in small quantities. Have your store a quick distributing station, not a warehouse. Find out what is the record turnover rate for your line of business and work to that end. Turnover will not only release capital and permit extension of business and increase sales, but will save many a dollar from that swallower of profit, 'Clearance Sale.' "[17]

Turnover varied according to department. Between 1896 (the first year stock turnover was measured) and 1906, sales increased from $3,165,934 to $5,317,340. Business almost doubled during that very prosperous ten-year period. On the other hand, the stock turnover rate remained relatively constant. Predictably, the grocery department had the most rapid turnover rate, varying from thirteen to eight times a year. The next highest turnover was in the wholesale dry goods department, which had numbers between eight and one-third and six times. Interestingly enough, clothing was "turned over" six times during the year rather than with the changing seasons. The hardware department experienced the least amount of change, which probably reflected as much as anything else the constancy of the product, turning over only three and one-quarter times in a single year.

Of course, volume of sales was the most sensitive monitor of general business conditions, buying habits of consumers, and whatever was new in the air. ZCMI had healthy sales in good times — particularly during wars — but in times of national depression sales plummeted. In Utah the agricultural, mining, and business sectors were inextricably linked, dependent on each other for support. When one or more of these suffered loss in terms of markets or resources, the others felt the effect.

This interconnectedness was poignantly evident in the crisis following the end of World War I. The rumblings of war in Europe spread across the great plains of the United States and like an angry whirlwind shook up business with a false high and subsequent drop. In April of 1915 the business forecast portended great disaster for Utah. Local conditions were shaky at best, distressed miners were laid off by the hundreds, and prices for agricultural products were on the decline because of increased mechanization. Yet less than a year later the tide had turned, surprising those predictors of doom who questioned the source of this newfound prosperity. "Whether it happened on account of the war or in spite of it, are puzzling questions, but the fact remains, that we have prospered in the midst of world-wide chaos."[18] This was largely due to a dramatic increase in prices that affected trade throughout the United States. A few examples: the price of epsom salts rose from 80 cents to $4.50 a pound, wool bags rose from $32.10 to $63.00 per hundred, and the cost of denim went from $9.50 to $17.50 a yard. These prices benefited merchants and penalized consumers, but generally helped to pump a new optimism and energy into the economy. Business at ZCMI reflected this optimism, as sales increased from $7,731,641 in 1916 to $9,931,867 in 1917, a jump of 20 percent. "Despite international complication, disappointing crops, labor troubles, and other adverse factors, general business attained record dimensions with prices and profits unprecedented."[19] But this hope proved to be false and as easily shattered as a piece of glass.

1920 was a year that went down in infamy in the history of Utah, "unwept, unhonored, and unsung. . . . It left all the most serious and vexatious problems which developed during the interval as a heritage, or a continuing influence for the coming months and years."[20] The depression following in the backlash of World War I was unparalleled in its intensity and the pervasiveness with which it swept all sections of the country. Prices of securities, commodities, raw materials, agricultural products, and manufactured wares plummeted, affecting every part of the economy. Utah was one of the hardest hit. The door to new markets and competition that had swung open during the war had just as quickly shut. In just one year, between 1920 and 1921, business at ZCMI fell 27 percent. By October 1921 prices in Salt

Lake City were at the 1912 level. It would not be until several years later that prices would reach the 1920 level again.

Just as rapid growth had required drastic changes in the company's operating methods, so did rapid decline. A letter of November 21, 1921, addressed to all department managers, acknowledged disastrous business conditions, declining prices, and lowered purchasing power of buyers. During the war the surplus and increased capitalized property was five times the prewar figure. Earnings available in 1921 for distribution needed to be one and one-half times larger than before the war for the company to break even. Taxes had increased, as had overhead. This combination of problems demanded that substantial and sweeping changes be made in the company's organization.

This letter and the series of discussions that followed attempted to evaluate the sales situation, asking what departments needed reorganization, where new traveling salesmen could supplement the sales force, or what departments should be eliminated altogether. In addition, Bennett created the position of sales auditor to oversee the necessary changes.

The depression of the 1920s was the only time during this thirty-year period that sales dipped at all. Despite seasonal fluctuations in the market, ZCMI's sales gradually increased to a high point in 1920 on the eve of the depression. Liabilities remained constant as did capitalization throughout the period. ZCMI mirrored the prosperity of the nation during the first years of the twentieth century, truly the beginning of something new.

In December 1926 Heber J. Grant recruited a fresh new talent to help pull ZCMI out of the grasp of the depression. William L. Walker was a Utah boy who had left the state for graduate studies at Harvard University's Graduate School of

Business Administration. A firm of management engineers and accountants in Boston had hired Walker fresh out of graduate school. His specialty was the reorganization of management methods for large manufacturing and merchandising companies. In 1922 a number of the companies reorganized by Walker merged as the Washburn Company of Worcester, Massachusetts. They elected their former consultant vice president of the newly created entity. Grant hoped that Walker could work the same miracles for ZCMI.

During that same year a series of talks broadcast on KSL radio recounted ZCMI's history and its particular contribution to the community. One attempted to pinpoint the company's influence on business in the region, a somewhat illusive quality that visitors to the store had tried to describe. They perceived a "spirit of unity that suggests one immense family, an influence or a something manifest but indefinable to them that they had not observed in any other store which they have visited in their travels."[21] The editor of the *ZCMI Advocate*, Henry Halton, described it as an "invisible something that if we will catch the spirit of it is an incentive that makes its impress upon the purchaser, the salesperson, or the official of the concern." In typical Mormon fashion he saw it as a "soul and from it emanates that unseen influence."

Another evening's broadcast sought the answer in another source—the employee handbook. Company direction given to employees about personal conduct reflected these lofty notions. "You are working for an Institution which stands for the highest ideals and you are expected to maintain this standard in your personal lives. Otherwise you will not advance with the organization."[22]

While the nation's youth in the 1920s were reveling in the newfound freedom of the postwar years, ZCMI was no longer the temporal arm of The Church of Jesus Christ of Latter-day Saints. The institution had indulged in trade with the Gentile world in unheard-of proportions. Products were regularly marketed that would have scandalized the company's founders. Yet the company was still at least self-consciously aware that it was different, a part of the world, yet apart. Defining that position with its newly commercialized identity would continue to occupy both leaders and patrons of the institution during the middle years of the twentieth century.

NOTES

1. Letter from Heber J. Grant to the Board of Directors, ZCMI History file.
2. *ZCMI Advocate* 8:41.
3. Minutes of the Board of Directors, Volume F, April 5, 1921, p. 296.
4. ZCMI Payroll, 1907.
5. *ZCMI Advocate* 8:106.
6. *ZCMI Advocate* 6:13.
7. Hazel Youngberg, "Child Labor in Utah" (Master's thesis, University of Utah, 1907).
8. Minutes of the Board of Directors, Volume F, June 17, 1920, p. 276.
9. Ibid., December 21, 1922, p. 333.
10. Ibid., Volume E, March 19, 1903, p. 331.
11. Ibid., Volume F, June 8, 1922, p. 325.
12. Ibid., Volume E, February 21, 1901, p. 237.
13. Ibid.
14. Report of Management, May 18, 1922.
15. *ZCMI Advocate* 5:39.
16. Ibid., p. 90.
17. Ibid., p. 50.
18. Minutes of the Board of Directors, Volume F, February 17, 1916, p. 180.
19. Ibid., February 15, 1917, p. 204.
20. Ibid., February 28, 1917, p. 287.
21. *ZCMI Advocate* 11:230.
22. Ibid., p. 247.

Z.C.M.i.

MODERNIZATION
1930–1960

ZCMI'S INTERCONNECTEDNESS with the world outside
was never as clear as during the great depression—a decade
when Americans everywhere began to experience what had
been in Utah a reality since the spring of 1921. As ZCMI
struggled to survive the postwar slump in business it met a
second tempest head-on: a depression unparalleled in scope
and severity. ZCMI's reaction to the depression typified that
of the state at large as the company responded to human
suffering, unionization, and the encroaching power of the
federal government into the private sector. Three central
themes marked this era: (1) the drive for self-determinism,
(2) economy in wage and hour cutbacks, and (3) the push
for recovery to the prewar levels of prosperity.

In 1931 ZCMI's parent store was still located in the center

of Salt Lake City's downtown business district. The wholesale warehouse was a few blocks to the west on 42 South and 2nd West. Other warehouses, a central delivery garage, and branch stores stretched across the valley and throughout the state.

Crowds of unemployed miners roamed the wide streets of Salt Lake City's business district, bumping shoulders with men distracted by important work to be done. To the unemployed, any work seemed significant. The depression hit Utah like a bitter and shocking slap, hurling its ugly spite on up to 35.8 percent of the state's adult workers who could not find any work. Those who did work earned on the average $300 a year, a figure only 80 percent of the national average. Wages were cut back even more rapidly than work hours.

Sales in downtown department stores were down 40 percent in 1931. The retail food price index, which had fallen 37 percent, failed to match the 45 percent drop in per capita income. In Utah an extraordinary number of people — 206 out of every 1,000—received government funds or support from private charities. Only three states had more citizens on relief.

Many of those on relief were farmers stunned by two severe droughts — first in 1931 and again in 1934—that rendered their land useless and dashed any hope for a rapid recovery from the depression. The state benefited from programs of the first New Deal, such as the Agricultural Adjustment Administration, which pumped more than $10,000,000 in direct payments into Utah's economy. Its effect was quickly noted by the unemployed, who once again become consumers. In 1932 ZCMI's sales increased by 32 percent and began a steady move toward their pre-1920 levels. Branch store sales in rural areas increased even more dramatically, by 52 percent. Retail sales were the best in five years in Salt Lake City during the

Christmas of 1933. Improvements in employment, business, and per capita income promised a brighter future.

As in the 1920s, ZCMI's first reaction to the depression was to cut employees' wages and hours. Everyone was affected by these cutbacks; even management shared a 10 percent cut in salaries. The vice chair of the Mutual Aid Society, when dismissed in 1938, bemoaned the severity of the unfortunate series of cuts he had endured during the early thirties:

> Under the depression, which was during Mr. Walker's time I suffered a cut in wages of $35.00. Later in 1931 my son being called on a mission to Holland which required the salary I then received, I inquired of Mr. Walker if there was danger of another cut. He assured me there was not. My son had been in the field but one month when I received another cut of $30.00 the amount needed to keep the boy in the field. This worked a real hardship upon me and necessitated the help of others.[1]

During the New Deal some salaries actually increased because of National Recovery Administration fair price and wage codes. For example, girl apprentices little satisfied with the $9.00 they received weekly had another $1.50 to spend. Regular salesladies were pleased as well with the jump from $12.00 to $13.00 a week. Others were exempt from these increases; valets who parked customers' cars still received 30 cents an hour, and waitresses scrapped by with 28 cents each hour.

Salaries reflected the series of guidelines and provisions set by the NRA, which imposed minimum wage and maximum hour standards upon the retail industry. The Forty-Four Hour Federal Labor Law passed by the Utah legislature followed a legislative trend throughout the country toward shorter hours and in some cases increases in base wages.

ZCMI reacted to the threat these measures seemed to pose by joining forces with other members of the Retail Merchants Bureau of Salt Lake City in a legal battle against conformity.

The Wage and Hour Bill centered on two basic issues: reduced hours and increased minimum wages. Those who studied the bill anticipated a cost for ZCMI of at least $15,000 in salary increases for employees in the wholesale, delivery, hardware, grocery, and appliance divisions. Cutting back the forty-eight-hour work week to forty-two-and-one-half hours would mean that a number of additional employees would have to be hired, increasing the amount of benefits paid by the company. (Retail employees already worked the lesser number of hours.)

Mandatory Orders Two and Three of the State Industrial Commission went a step further in April 1940 when they established a base pay rate of $15.00 a week for "well selected and well trained" employees. Delivery boys under eighteen years of age who had work permits from the Board of Education were the only exceptions; they were to be paid not less than 20 cents an hour or $8.00 a week. Based on 1937 payroll figures, this increase would be $12,386 and would include retail and wholesale employees alike. Because of the unique combined control of the organization of both retail and wholesale, ZCMI was subject to interstate commerce law.

Financial issues in this particular case, although significant, were not the only important concerns. The issue of self-determination—the overriding belief that business should thrive independent of governmental control—had increased in importance. ZCMI joined forces with competitors Auerbach's, Keith O'Brien, Penney's, and Sears to fight this common foe, hiring the law firm Ray, Quinney, and Nebekker to wage the legal battle. ZCMI itself paid $1,050 for its part in the proceedings. The merchandisers were successful in this instance in forestalling what would prove to be the inevitable.

In the 1930s a second common enemy of retailers showed its forbidding face in the form of the union. The provisions of Section 7a of the NRA gave labor unions a long-needed legitimacy and power. Labor leaders seized the moment and spoke before workers across the nation, combining the rhetoric of unionization and nationalism and using the NRA as proof that President Roosevelt wanted workers to join. Laborers in Utah rallied to the cry, and in one year union membership jumped from 965 members in 27 separate unions to 5,926 in 71.[2] Between 1933 and 1935 union membership in Utah increased six times. Mechanics, factory employees, taxi drivers, and finally salespeople were organized.

But again, resistance to unionization by ZCMI's management was more complicated than the economic penalties it promised. The Mormon church had a tradition of opposition to unionization and in particular the closed shop, "because this means the denial of the divine right to work. It is not necessary for the protection of labor and sets up a labor tyranny which too often falls under the direction of concepts, ideals, and pernicious practices foreign to the American way of life."

To the Church unionization was divisive. It was a harbinger of disunion— dissension between saints. "No true patriot can foster, promote, or take part in any such activities or in any organization making use of them." Furthermore, "No church member can engage in such activities and partake of the lawlessness and hatred incident thereto and yet maintain in his heart the spirit of the Master without which no one has the righteous life." One final statement could have easily been ZCMI's motto throughout this fight: "Honor and strength to those workers—men and women—who stand stoutly and persistently against these subversive influences."[3]

ZCMI's wholesale division was always a world apart from the retail store. It was here that the company's first union was organized. In 1937 the "Wholesale Employees Organization" voiced both lofty and practical ideals: "to promote better understanding of the department's needs tomorrow, to increase loyalty in the institution, to work for increased patronage, to work out wage issues."[4] Again, the wholesale division was the first to feel the effects of NRA regulations because of federal interstate commerce jurisdiction. When the United States Supreme Court unilaterally swept away the NRA in 1935 the Wagner Act took up the slack in the battle for collective bargaining.

In December the CIO union approached the ZCMI Wholesale Employees Organization with the idea of association. Ensuing negotiations were stalemated by two irreconcilable issues: "1) the demand by the union for a form of closed shop designated by them as a maintenance of membership clause; which issue management absolutely refused to consider and 2) the Union's demand that acts of the management in hiring, firing, or promoting of employees be subject to question by the Union and to compulsory arbitration by a third party."[5] This second issue again centered on the notion of self-determination. Because ZCMI was primarily responsible to its stockholders, The Church of Jesus Christ of Latter-day Saints, and its employees, answering to a union seemed to be out of the question. Because of an already complicated relationship with the Church, management was committed to staying clear of any other outside control. Both issues were further complicated because of the supervisory jurisdiction of the War Labor Board during 1942.

In May 1949 the issue of unionization surfaced again when John Kelly, organizing agent for the American Federation of Labor Teamsters Union, Local 222 of Salt Lake City, convinced fourteen of the nineteen truck drivers of ZCMI's delivery fleet to push the idea of membership in Teamsters. Kelly was a slick-talking, thirty-five-year-old wonder salesman selling the promise of increased wage rates and postwar stabilization of employment. Teamsters set their sights on all unorganized workers in the city, realizing that "the city would probably fall (quickly) after successful organization of ZCMI drivers."[6]

The *Salt Lake Tribune* ran an editorial on May 24, 1952, that voiced the concerns of the teamster drivers at ZCMI, who typically earned $1.30 an hour. "Dear Utah Citizen:" it began, "What Would You Do? Twenty eight drivers at ZCMI's Teamsters Union have tried to get a written agreement. All teamsters want is a living wage—a written agreement that guarantees the normal security that goes with any job."[7] Management was unfaltering in its fight against unionization.

The devaluation of ZCMI stock was a final retrenchment measure in response to the depression. William Walker and the executive committee of the board of directors discussed this last-ditch measure for a number of months before it occurred. Walker passionately supported the idea, suggesting stock (which had a current value of $150) be returned to a par value of $50. This seemingly extraordinary measure reflected the severity of the financial climate and how badly it had shaken the company's chief executives. Walker suggested three changes be made: (1) adjust the capitalization of the company to more nearly accord with the value of the investment, (2) prevent a deficit from appearing on the books, and (3) adjust the values of capital assets to more fairly represent present-day values.[8]

No program of the New Deal eradicated the misery and confusion caused by the depression. But ironically, a second World War did. Wartime spending lifted Utah's economy and energized the state's manufacturing sector.

ZCMI was throughout the war years the model citizen, sponsoring war bond drives, supporting supply conservation and salvage efforts, and aiding in the production of uniforms for men and women of the United States Army corps. ZCMI's response when called upon for help was enthusiastic and generous.

In April 1942 the company's merchandising management under the direction of Harold H. Bennett adapted to war conditions and proposed four new policies: (1) a policy against gambling in merchandise stocks, (2) well-balanced, fresh inventories, (3) cooperation with the government in every way, and (4) payroll deduction plans for purchasing bonds and defense stamps.[9] Sales immediately reflected the increased activity in the business community caused by the war, jumping in 1942 by 15.1 percent.

Just two weeks after the bombing of Pearl Harbor and America's entrance into World War II, ZCMI joined in raising money for the American Red Cross War Fund. The group challenged ZCMI to raise $125,000 of the projected $50 million earmarked to "meet the essential needs of our armed forces and to look after the welfare of their families, and to relieve distress and suffering of the civilian population in regions, where as in the Hawaiian Islands and the Philippines, the treacherous attack of the enemy already has wrought destruction and suffering."

ZCMI joined other local businesses "to keep America on an even keel. It is our job to face the future courageously. Let us show the boys in service that we are behind them 100 percent."

Assistant manager Harold H. Bennett first met with representatives of the treasury department in Los Angeles in September of 1942 about the proposed war bond campaign at a mandatory gathering of members of the retail and theater industries. Representatives of the eleven western states were given responsibility for selling one billion dollars' worth of defense stamps and bonds each month for the rest of the year. ZCMI was asked to "lead in the drive to sell bonds and stamps, not only to every employee of the company but to customers who enter our store."[10]

Soon ZCMI offered bonds as sales incentives, bonuses to employees, lures to entice customers into the store. A "Miss War Bond Queen" contest held during the 7th War Loan Drive brought in thousands of dollars; the purchase of an individual bond cast a vote for a favored contestant. The "lovely Miss June Gorringe," ZCMI's candidate for the crown, received 2,000 separate votes at a value of $127,218 that put her in third place.[11]

Policies of the War Industries Board also affected ZCMI. Conservation of building materials, rubber tires, and automobile supplies stalemated any improvements in physical facilities or the delivery fleet. Tires and tubes in both wholesale and retail were rationed and periodically taken off the market entirely. In March 1945 management created a reserve fund to secure funds for postwar projects. This was necessary to earmark reserves for improvements delayed by wartime restrictions on construction and new equipment.

When the government created the Civilian Motor Transportation Western Defense Command in 1945, it mobilized a backup system of civilian transportation for times of emergency. ZCMI's delivery fleet was on constant alert, accessible on demand for the transport of army supplies.

Restrictions on manpower penalized ZCMI as well. After September 1, 1944, governmental regulations prohibited the hiring of any new male employee who was not a discharged war veteran. Despite the critical nature of the manpower problem at the company, the War Manpower Commission considered neither retail nor wholesale operations a top priority. Despite this ZCMI had an unprecedented 1,565 employees, including large numbers of women handling traditionally male departments.

Advertising emphasized patriotism and support of national conservation programs during these years. ZCMI was very much the good citizen's store. Programs like that created by the Supply, Conservation, and Salvage Committee, "The S.O.S. — Save on Supplies — Defense Comes First," encouraged employees and customers alike to willingly adjust to wartime restrictions.

After the war the ZCMI clothing factory had a surplus of 561 army nurse uniforms worth $5,000 that became obsolete with the end of fighting. "We took the buttons off of some of the dresses and attempted to use the dresses for elevator uniforms and for other purposes. We were notified by the Army that this was a violation of the uniform regulations and we would not be permitted to dispose of these dresses unless every trace of military identification was removed — including the braid."[12]

Despite losses incurred, inconvenience, and adjustments demanded by various programs, the war had an overwhelmingly positive effect on ZCMI. Business doubled during

World War II and would only improve during the next two decades. No soldier who left ZCMI to serve in the war was killed. When they returned they came home to a business that had grown and changed.

ZCMI had mirrored the country's efforts to use the New Deal to recoup its losses felt during the depression; in turn, ZCMI's response to the war in Europe typified the best in America. The man who led the company during these interesting years was known for his size, for his warmth, and for his shrewdness at business. Above all else he taught that it was people who were important.[13]

Richard W. Madsen, known as R.W., came from a long tradition in the furniture business. At age fourteen he first worked in his father, Peter Madsen's, store. When his parents traveled to Denmark on a genealogical research trip they left sixteen-year-old Richard behind to manage the family business. His forty-year career at Madsen's and later Standard Furniture was a rewarding one. He would later remark:

> The furniture industry is one of the most fascinating businesses that exists. A successful merchant in his endeavor has no remorse of conscience. He has given people better surroundings, enhanced the longing for the beautiful things of life; aided in holding a happy family together, and taught thrift thru installment selling. It seems difficult to deviate from this vocation after once embracing its joys.[14]

It would be only after much cajoling that Madsen would be convinced to deviate even in part from this business. ZCMI was located immediately south of Standard Furniture, which was in 1933 the largest-volume furniture store per square foot in the nation.

The president of Standard Furniture, R.W. Madsen, and the president of the Mormon church, Heber J. Grant, were close personal friends. ZCMI was losing a great deal of money under the management of William Walker during the Depression years. Explanations vary as to why. Nevertheless, President Grant frequently asked his friend Madsen to help save the company by becoming its manager. Madsen was already on the board of directors of the company; he was, in fact, on the boards of most of the Church-owned businesses. Madsen was a part of any business associated with the Church or with Grant. At the time he had seventeen different directorships in real estate, banking, hotel, and retail organizations, besides running his own successful business, which was and would continue to be his top priority. Grant finally cornered R.W. with the proposition that Madsen consider it a "calling" to help save ZCMI, therein adding an additional and irresistible test of his loyalty to the Church. Through subsequent negotiations it was agreed that Madsen could potentially run both his own business and ZCMI.

And this is what he did. Beginning a long day at Standard Furniture at 7:00 A.M., Madsen would walk afternoons next door to his office on the third floor of ZCMI. The executive office had Madsen's big mahogany desk and a table for the assistant manager.

Madsen and his assistant manager, Ashby Snow, were each paid $500 a month with an additional bonus of $10,000 to $15,000 at the end of the year. Madsen was generally credited with initiating the modernization process at ZCMI, which was marked as much as anything by a more centralized operation. This centralization was accomplished by a tightening of control over branches and wholesale divisions, an increase in upper-management personnel, and improvements in accounting and record keeping. Richard Madsen's personal records and those of the businesses he led were immaculate and reflect the exacting standards he imposed

Richard W. Madsen, general manager of ZCMI from 1933 to 1946.

upon his employees. He led the company with a good-humored authority.

Madsen was often seen walking down the aisles of the store leaning heavily on his cane, pausing to tease the elderly salesclerks, calling some by name, others by nicknames he used to make them blush with embarrassment. "Ginger," he would say to an eighty-year-old saleswoman, "you're the prettiest little flower on the selling floor." His family business professed a long tradition of personalized service, which he brought to ZCMI: "Operate simply and economically and give the customer his money's worth with personalized, friendly, leisurely service. Our men can and do call a large

97

percentage of their customers by name. Yet we make a new customer just as welcome. We want them back for the next generation."[15]

Sales more than doubled during the thirteen years Madsen served as manager of ZCMI, going from $8,492,735 annual value with a net worth of $5,579,427 in 1933 to $22,017,105 and $31,828,793 in 1945. In 1932, the year before he began, no dividends were paid, but by 1945 the company distributed $1,614,717 to stockholders.

When Richard Madsen resigned in April 1946 it was largely due to ill health. He was at the time the largest individual owner of stock in the company and would continue to wield power and influence as chair of the board.

In November 1933 Madsen first met with the company accountant, a young man who had already worked at the store for seven years and was the company secretary-treasurer and the son of former general manager John F. Bennett. Harold H. Bennett would, in the forty-seven years he worked at ZCMI, exert an unprecedented influence on the company. His personality, business philosophy, and management style would change the company, forcing it to confront the national retail market and to pull itself up to competitive twentieth-century standards of excellence.

In January 1936 Bennett became assistant manager, assuming more-than-full-time responsibilities from his table in the manager's office when Madsen was at Standard Furniture. Although he retained general supervision of the company's records, he was relieved of controller's duties. Instead he handled all retail and wholesale merchandising. When Madsen retired in 1946 Bennett was the logical choice for general manager in his own right.

Bennett had seen every aspect of the company's business

98

from the bottom up. As accountant, controller, secretary, treasurer, and assistant manager he had learned the business, understood its complexities, and made many friends throughout the store. *Business Week* magazine would call him both "suave and far-seeing," one *Woman's Wear Daily* editor found him "remarkably well-informed" about every aspect of the business. Bennett wore many hats at ZCMI, as controller, as general manager, and later president of the company in personnel, merchandising, and general management.[16]

Bennett quickly improved the structure of the organization and surrounded himself with loyal and supportive divisional managers. He had a sense of the importance of changing ZCMI from a pioneer aberration to one of the finest, most up-to-date, fashion-conscious department stores in the West. Bennett helped this to happen. He had a dream for ZCMI and he helped make that dream a reality. Harold Bennett began a longtime association with the National Retail Merchants Association in 1945; in 1962 and then again in 1963 he served as president of that prestigious organization. The important and continuing role he played in NRMA symbolized the reaching out he envisioned for ZCMI.

During Bennett's first month as manager, Harry Nelson, formerly of Macy's, filled the newly created position of retail merchandise manager, Wendell Adams was appointed head of Personnel, and Bennett created a new position of sales promotion. Bennett attracted Dorothy Ennis from Marshall Field and Company to ZCMI in April 1949 to become the new Women's and Children's Apparel division manager, again a newly created position. In 1951 when Bennett made Ennis divisional merchandise manager of Ready-to-Wear, she was replaced by George Condie of Hale Bros. in San Francisco.

Marjorie Beard answered an ad for an "Executive Secretary, at least thirty years of age" in 1946. She easily won her way into the company (although she was only twenty-three), and by 1956 had become so indispensable that she was appointed assistant secretary of the company, the first woman in the United States to serve as an officer of a retail organization. She, like Bennett, had a sense of the importance of ZCMI to the community and with her friendly and devoted service made an important contribution in her years at ZCMI.[17]

Easily as important as who sat at the top of the company was who held up the bottom. Employees throughout the store felt the fair and equitable policies of Harold Bennett. He was known as a kind and gracious man who refused to impose himself upon anyone but preferred to stand back, letting his interest and his concern be known.

When Bennett became manager there were 1,248 employees who were paid a total $1,928,096 in wages. Ninety had worked between five and ten years at the store, forty-two between ten and fifteen years, eighty-one for fifteen to twenty-five years, and sixty-two for more than twenty-five years. Elderly employees were not forced into retirement but continued to work as they chose. Bennett let it be known that he valued their contribution, saying on one occasion, "An institution like ZCMI cannot be built with people who come and go."[18] He established a policy of recognizing employees with ten, fifteen, twenty, and twenty-five years of service. Eighty percent of those employees were protected by insurance purchased through the store.

The same year Bennett became manager, salaries began to rise after the War Production Board removed controls. In

1946 minimum wage did not apply to high school students. Girls and boys under age sixteen received 45 cents an hour. Teenage boys between sixteen and eighteen received 50 cents, yet girls still received only 45 cents. It would be many years before equitable pay scales would be established at ZCMI. Adult beginners were another exempt category, men receiving 65 cents and women again receiving a lower wage of 50 cents.

Until the late 1940s all hiring and firing passed before the preview of the manager, who knew most employees and their particular talents and responsibilities. A feeling of family prevailed when management and everyone else knew each other and communicated daily in the store.

This feeling of camaraderie and goodwill was facilitated at social gatherings as well. Bennett was a great one to organize parties for his employees. Each month as a sales incentive the retail selling personnel who exceeded their sales quota could enjoy a relaxing afternoon, dinner, and evening of Bingo at the Homestead resort. But the most coveted prize of all was a ride to Antelope Island on Bennett's boat, the *Halcyon*. The legendary halcyon was a bird who nested on the sea about the time of the winter solstice and calmed the waves. After arriving at the island, while the boat rested at anchor Mr. Bennett and Mr. Dean Williams donned tall white chef's hats and aprons to serve a delicious dinner that had been prepared in the Tiffin Room kitchen. Bennett was a halcyon himself, whose quiet, elegant presence calmed waves and forestalled the storm.

The employees' Mutual Aid Society continued to lend assistance to those with problems, although one benefit, the Doctor's Club, was discontinued in December 1933 because of numerous complaints from doctors in the community who saw it as an "unjust practice against their profession."[19]

Management sponsored a number of classes and special events to entertain and educate, thrill and improve the minds of the employees of ZCMI. At 6:00 P.M. on March 9, 1938, all retail employees met in the newly opened, redecorated tearoom to enjoy a nice dinner and see the highlights of the Amos Parrish Fashion Clinic. Ideally, Bennett believed, "it will prove beneficial to them in helping them sell our fashion merchandise and making them style conscious."[20] Bennett kept close contact with the Parrish Fashion Office in New York, insisting that ZCMI present the most current styles.

One of the most extravagant displays was staged in 1937 in the midst of the depression.

> Our importation of Paris models arrived here and were on exhibit in the French Room. 500 visitors inspecting these gowns. The entire cost of this merchandise including transportation costs, was $728.50, and there is no doubt but that these dresses will be sold, but probably not at the price marked as they vary in price from $198 to $498. We will, however, get cost out of the merchandise, and we are of the opinion it was a splendid advertising idea as nearly all the richer class of Salt Lake visited our store for the purpose of viewing these gowns.[21]

Obviously, in a city where the average annual income was $398, few could actually purchase a French gown priced at almost $500, but everyone could dream. Models in the spring fashion show displayed gowns almost anyone could hope to buy.

Fashion was always important to the ladies, as Brigham Young noted early on, but after World War II fashion would become an increasingly important part of ZCMI's identity in the community. ZCMI became a fashion leader, and for many an arbiter of taste and style.

ZCMI served as one of *Mademoiselle* magazine's college fashion headquarters.

One employee manual of the 1950s encouraged sales personnel to be fashion conscious. To help make this possible, employees were given a 15 percent discount on all purchases. The manual asked that most important question, "How do you look today?" Apparently, the person who looked right knew what look was right. Information was given liberally in employee pamphlets, like "Off to Work," the ZCMIRROR, and other in-house publications. Before World War II all female employees were required to wear dresses of "modest styling" in either black or navy. Although later a greater variety was encouraged, occasionally the dark colors again became fashionable. "The colors selected by your dress committee as appropriate to the season are black or navy blue. Solid colors are preferred at all times."[22]

As early as 1940 ZCMI was chosen by *Mademoiselle* magazine as one of its college fashion headquarters. During the 1950s high school fashion board representatives competed in the Joyce-Jantzen Jamboree to become Miss ZCMI. The *Mademoiselle* College Show, a *Glamour* magazine show, and the

Amos Parrish Fall Fashion review filled the autumn months with exciting fashion events.

ZCMI was "the Utopia for brides-to-be." In the Bride Shop, Besse Springer, bridal consultant, answered questions about everything from wedding rings to tuxedos for the bride-groom. Refreshments for wedding parties could be purchased in the candy department; Marjorie Turner of the linen department coordinated trousseau lines; the best in china, crystal, and silver were available through the Wedding Gift Registry. "When a bride comes to ZCMI, everybody breaks their darn necks to see that each bride has the most thrilling, most beautiful, most individual wedding that can be devised."[23]

Even the youngest customers were attracted to the store by impressive visitors from afar. The annual visit of Santa Claus became even more thrilling in 1936 when Santa descended from the sky in a helicopter. As he visited with excited young guests he handed out 1,000 miniature airplanes donated by United Airlines. That same year for just 25 cents a child could experience the wonders of outer space at the "Buck Rogers" booth opened in the children's sales area.

For those more studious shoppers who were less impressed by the latest fashions, the book department offered weekly book reviews. One held for a crowd of twenty women on the afternoon of January 5, 1937, had as a subject the new romantic best-selling novel *Gone With the Wind*.

A myriad of customer services were offered to satisfy one's every need: art and needlework instruction for the creatively inclined, repair for sporting goods, dry cleaning, packing and mailing services, shoe repair and polishing, a circulating library, and wardrobe planning, among many others. Management was so committed to a service concept that they offered cash bonuses for the best suggestions for special services.

Employees could browse or borrow books from the store's library, which included such titillating titles as *Proceedings of the Constitutional Convention for the State of Utah*, *Bancroft's Histories*, and *Economics for Executives* (a series of twenty-four texts that provided practical interpretations of principles of economics and business).

As ZCMI's services became more complicated, often exotic, the business organization itself became increasingly centralized, streamlined, and specialized. One step toward centralization was the sale of the remaining cooperatives that had struggled to stay in business for so many years. When the Cedar Mercantile closed in July 1931 it faced, as had many others before, two alternatives: (1) to sell its real estate, merchandise, and operations to ZCMI, or (2) to allow the stockholders of Cedar Merc to retain the real estate but let ZCMI rent the store and operate the business. Two months after Cedar closed its doors the Blackfoot Mercantile chose another alternative and turned its entire business over to ZCMI to satisfy its debt of $6,000.

The inventory of the Kanab store was more difficult to dispose of. Next to the dry goods on the shelves sat Indian relics; old skulls, bones, baskets, and even a mummified child that had been traded for goods waited for just the right buyer.[24]

In 1935 Rueul Phillips, manager of the branch stores, proposed that ZCMI close all stores that did less than $100,000 a year in business, particularly those that could not be operated at a profit. Phillips pointed to two principal reasons why branch stores had done so poorly: competition of chain stores, and the decline in wholesale dry goods volume. Improved transportation connecting rural Utah to the big city put others out of business. Those cooperatives that did survive the automobile caved in to the insurmountable problems of the depression.

By June Phillips had conducted a sweeping study of the network of branch stores, finding that ZCMI's seventeen branch stores represented a $517,099 investment. During the past five years the company had lost $473,000 on that investment. Phillips believed that a forced liquidation would cost $150,000, increasing the loss even further. Instead, he proposed, let each store close as desired.[25]

Despite the failure of many local cooperatives, overall sales steadily increased during Bennett's years as general manager. Between 1940 and 1950 sales increased three times, profits three and one-half times, and taxes five. Dividends on stocks increased two times and the net worth of the company rose one and one-half times.

The invasion of South Korea created another brief period of scare buying, but it did not have the scope or magnitude that accompanied the World War II period. The linen department, for instance, reported unprecedented increases in sales of sheets and pillowcases. Nylon hosiery, blankets, knit underwear, and electric appliances all reported up to seven times the normal business and virtually exhausted inventories.[26] President Truman asked retailers to cooperate with his economic plan on three different ideas: (1) that materials for national security be available at need, (2) that every attempt be made to prevent hoarding, and (3) that taxes be boosted to combat inflationary pressures.[27] The postwar "red fear" touched even ZCMI, as company employees were invited to hear Cleon Skousen speak on the threat of communism at the Assembly Hall on November 11, 1953.

During the first year of fighting in Korea—from June 12, 1951—all ZCMI's wholesale concerns were unified under one roof in the remodeled Remington Small Arms Plant space, which had been purchased after the war. Advertised as "America's First One-Stop Wholesale Center," this expansive space made it possible to display 75,000 separate items. "Mountaineer," "Miss Mountaineer," and "Big Hunter" overalls were displayed in this same building with "speed, efficiency, and class." The next year R.W. Maycock was chosen the first manager of the Wholesale Center.

In the beginning the wholesale division was at the center of ZCMI's network of cooperatives and branch stores. The retail store accounted for only a small part of overall sales. During the early years of the depression wholesale departments sold four times more than the retail store—out of a total $13,036,026 in sales, $8,950,991 was from Wholesale and $3,585,319 was from the main store, including both the upstairs and the basement budget store. In 1929 ZCMI was still overwhelmingly a wholesale house and realized its most stable profits from these divisions. The clothing factory, which was part of the wholesale division, sold $304,101 worth of overalls for men, women and children in 1929. Contract departments accounted for $37,140, a very small part of the total. The wholesale grocery was by far the most important part of the wholesale business, contributing one-third of the total sales, or $4,611,570; hardware was the next highest department with $1,357,395.

Wholesale had lower operating costs as well. Retail goods were much more expensive to market. Again in 1929, only $650 was spent on advertising for the wholesale grocery, and another $5,043 on a special promotional campaign—significantly less than the $110,142 spent by retail on advertising.

In 1929 there was an unprecedented amount of newspaper advertising for the basement store. Advertising was crucial to make ZCMI's retail store competitive, while the wholesale business was still able to hold its own with very little output. Total salaries for all departments were $983,890; those for the wholesale grocery were only $88,829. For every dollar paid in wages in the company as a whole, thirteen dollars' worth of goods were sold; in the wholesale grocery department the ratio was one to fifty-one.

By 1945 this basic relationship between retail and wholesale divisions had changed very little. Out of a total sales figure of $22,017,105, retail was responsible for $8,404,656; wholesale grocery, $9,166,569; other wholesale departments, $4,286,870; and the clothing factory, $159,007. The clothing factory suffered the largest dip in sales and was down 50 percent. Wholesale grocery was up to 41 percent of total sales.

But like so much in business, wholesaling was dramatically changed during the postwar years. Chain stores, buying groups, and consolidated buying plans forced many wholesale companies out of business.

The idea for liquidating the wholesale grocery division of ZCMI was first discussed in board meetings in early April 1952. Bennett thought that this would free up needed capital for expansion for the rest of the store. Between 1934 and 1950 wholesale accounted for 40 percent of sales and 34 percent of capital, but the profits produced by wholesale business were only 13.5 percent. Bennett's patience and commitment to expansion and growth can be seen over the next several years, during which time it became obvious that the world had changed so as to make ZCMI's wholesale business obsolete. It became evident that capital tied up in wholesale could more efficiently be utilized elsewhere.

During that same time the board changed the value of capital stock from $3,000,000 to its pre-1929 value of $6,000,000. This was accomplished by reducing the surplus stock from 5,757,139 to 2,821,289 and awarding a 100–percent stock dividend.

In 1953, after having lost money for five years on the clothing factory, the company shut it down. Stiff competition from a much more specialized market made it impossible to stay afloat. ZCMI's factory girls made children's "All-Overs," the ever-popular "Daisy Ann" dresses, and the "famous stop-loss" pockets of Mountaineer Overalls for the last time.

These measures were accomplished only through careful negotiation. Bennett worked with an essentially conservative, for the most part elderly, board, resistant to change and definitely cautious due to the lessons of the depression. Nevertheless, the idea for closing down the wholesale division began to make more sense as business continued to drop due to incredible new types of competition. The company lost 6 percent in 1957 and 3 percent in 1958 in wholesale departments.

After April 1958 Harold H. Bennett directed the company as president, the first president who was not also president of the Church. This was an overwhelming vote of confidence in his abilities and trust in his judgment. The Church of Jesus Christ of Latter-day Saints had become so large and complex in the 1950s that it was increasingly impossible for the Church president to be himself involved in each business with Church connections. Therefore, the First Presidency decided to each take separate assignments to work with company presidents, along with apostles who would serve on boards and act as intermediaries between the two bodies. J. Reuben Clark was for many years a key advisor and friend to Bennett

Harold H. Bennett, president of ZCMI from 1958 to 1973.

at ZCMI. His acute insight and knowledge made him the perfect addition to the board.

During 1959 Bennett began negotiations with Strevell-Patterson for the purchase of the wholesale hardware inventories; other companies proposed purchasing the stock of other wholesale departments. By April 1960 the board decided to close the three major wholesale departments, which were 60 percent liquidated already, to retire from wholesale entirely, and to expand operations with the capital released from wholesale. In a letter to employees Bennett announced this decision: "ZCMI is on the threshold of a great expansion program in its retail operation." He mentioned the new Cottonwood store, increased space in the new Kennecott building, and an expanded school and office supply division as particular projects that needed funds to grow. He believed growth would be made possible through capital obtained from the liquidation of wholesale rather than an increase in the capital structure of the company.

The year 1960 would be a turning point for ZCMI. Closing the wholesale division was a major factor in that change, a movement away from the past that made the future possible—a future replete with the promise of expanded and more diversified business.

NOTES

1. Executive Committee Minutes, letter, September 9, 1938.

2. Dee Scorup, "A History of Organized Labor in Utah" (Master's thesis, University of Utah, 1935), p. 12.

3. James R. Clark, ed., *Messages of the First Presidency*, 6 vols. (Salt Lake City: Bookcraft, 1963), 6:131, September 26, 1941.

4. Executive Committee Minutes, July 20, 1937.

5. Report of Management, May 24, 1944.

6. Ibid.

7. *Salt Lake Tribune*, May 24, 1952.

8. Executive Committee Minutes, letter from William Walker to Board, November 1, 1932.

9. Minutes of the Board of Directors, Volume G, April 4, 1942, p. 111.

10. Executive Committee Minutes, letter from E.O. Howard, General Chair of the Red Cross, to ZCMI, December 27, 1941.

11. Report of Management, September 23, 1942.

12. Report of Management, March 5, 1947.

13. *Salt Lake Tribune*, January 26, 1969.

14. Files of R.W. Madsen, p. 4.

15. *Salt Lake Tribune*, January 26, 1969.

16. Interview with Marjorie Beard by Martha Bradley, September 9, 1988, Salt Lake City, Utah.

17. ZCMIRROR, June 1956.

18. ZCMIRROR, August 1957.

19. Report of Management, December 30, 1933.

20. Report of Management, March 9, 1938.

21. Executive Committee Minutes, 1936, p. 338.
22. "And So To Work," 1955 Employee Handbook, ZCMI.
23. ZCMIRROR, June 1955.
24. Report of Management, November 6, 1933.
25. Report of Management, June 17, 1936.
26. Report of Management, July 19, 1950.
27. Ibid.

EXPANSION
1962–1986

THE AIR WAS CRISP AND FRESH on March 26, 1962. President Harold H. Bennett stood on a platform built for the dedication of the new Cottonwood branch of ZCMI. Next to him were Church president David O. McKay, apostle Le-Grand Richards, and other executives of the company, including the new store manager, Joseph Anderson. Bright splashes of color framed this prodigious gathering of Church and business leaders, thanks to planters filled with spring flowers: hyacinths and tulips of brilliant red, yellow, and orange. The west entrance itself was draped with stripes of colored ribbons in peach, white, and lime green. When Bennett stepped to the microphone and welcomed the crowd gathered in the west parking lot of the new Cottonwood Mall, he spoke of the many years of planning and preparation for

113

LDS Church President David O. McKay and ZCMI President Harold H. Bennett cut the ribbon opening the new Cottonwood Mall store.

that moment. It had taken almost eight years to study, plan, design, construct, and equip the new store, he said. Quietly finishing, he added, "We hope you like it as much as we loved preparing it."[1]

When President McKay cut the ribbons and pushed open the grand doors of this first major branch store in the twentieth century, it was the beginning of a new era for the company—one of unprecedented expansion that would in the next twenty years multiply sales and profits many times over,

ZCMI's Cottonwood Mall store opened in March of 1962.

increase the number of stores to eight by 1985, and spread ZCMI's business over a larger geographic area than ever.

Capital required for the scale and scope of Bennett's plans for the expansion of ZCMI became available after the sale of the downtown store to Zions Securities Corporation — a move that served the best interests of both the company and The Church of Jesus Christ of Latter-day Saints. It became apparent as early as 1956 that Zions Securities Corporation was consolidating properties in the blocks surrounding Church headquarters. At that time ZCMI's board of directors approved an option agreement permitting the sale of the Standard Furniture Company property and the Manx Building property on South Temple, with the provision that ZCMI would receive space in the projected Kennecott Building. During the next four years negotiations continued over how much and what that space would be. Throughout these dis-

115

cussions the idea often surfaced of demolishing the store altogether and building a new, updated building in its place. By May 1960 it was obvious to members of the board that the First Presidency of the LDS Church wanted all property around Church headquarters—including that of ZCMI.

Bennett announced publicly the intention of Zions Securities Corporation to buy ZCMI's physical facilities on May 16, 1960.

> The LDS Church has asked ZCMI to sell to it all the land presently containing its retail department store building in order that the Church may have perpetual control over the use of this land so near the Church headquarters Block. ZCMI would lease back this land on a long-term (30 year) lease with an option to renew for another thirty years at a basis of four percent per annum plus property taxes and assessments. The agreed sale price is $1,460,000. This property is on ZCMI's books at $212,430 and this sale will result in a capital gains tax of $311,893 leaving ZCMI a net gain of $935,677.[2]

A year later, in May 1961, Harold Bennett hired the architectural firm of Lorenzo S. Young and Partners to design a new building for the downtown location. After yet another year Victor Bruen and Associates was commissioned to completely restudy the property utilization of Block 75.

Finally, five years later, after continuous study and planning, the architects and economic consultants of the Block 75 project presented to the board plans and economic forecasts for a complete two-level, enclosed, air-conditioned shopping mall in the interior of Block 75 Downtown Salt Lake City with access to South Temple, Main, State, and First South streets. This impressive plan included two underground parking levels, two shopping levels above ground, and four parking levels above the shops, with parking space for about 2,000 cars total. A seventh parking level would be added in 1987.

Demolition for the new ZCMI Mall in downtown Salt Lake City began in 1967.

An impressive new ZCMI store of an unprecedented 368,000 square feet would anchor the projected shopping center. The mall itself would have 200,000 square feet of rentable shop space and an adjoining office tower with an additional 261,000 square feet. To keep ZCMI open for business during construction the project was carefully conceived in two phases—each approximately two years in duration. The idea had grown from its inception to include virtually an entire city block, the resources of the Church and other investors, and support of a combination of companies with ZCMI.

By 1967 demolition for the project had already commenced. At the same time, Bennett looked toward expansion in another direction: north. After sixty years ZCMI returned to Ogden.

Between 1962 and 1966 a committee that had been formed to explore possible expansion north studied four potential sites for an Ogden branch of ZCMI. The idea was considered, and later rejected, of purchasing Bon Marche and eliminating potentially the largest competitor. Groups favoring one location or another lobbied for support, realizing that a new ZCMI could move the business center from one part of town to another.

Opponents of the proposed plan pointed to ZCMI's failed history in Ogden and darkly forecasted overexpansion into an already saturated market. But Bennett and the board of directors saw expansion as the key to growth of the company, and Ogden as the next logical step.

According to marketing studies, Ogden was actually the most underdeveloped area in the state in terms of retailing. Establishing a major branch of ZCMI in Ogden would stretch out yet another arm of the company, strengthening its competitive position as the dominant force among competitors in Utah. Furthermore, it was another reasonable and progressive use of the capital freed by the liquidation of ZCMI Wholesale and the sale of the downtown store.

Eventually proponents of a downtown Ogden location prevailed in their lobbying efforts and a site was settled upon at 2380 Washington Boulevard. The projected store would have 127,000 square feet of selling space (5,000 fewer than Cottonwood). Construction on the Ogden store progressed satisfactorily during the next year and a half despite a few rather dramatic setbacks (like the roof on the main building collapsing after a severe storm). The total cost of the final building—$2,187,600—exceeded the initial bid by 30 percent.

The new Ogden ZCMI store opened in 1967.

Glazed white brick faced the new ZCMI building, creating a striking addition to downtown Ogden. A parapet of metal baked with blue porcelain enamel capped the building with an elegant accent. Grand canopies formed of antique brass shaded the main show windows from the summer sun. Customers entered the store through a formal garden court filled with flowers that changed with the seasons.

The grand opening of this second branch store took place in March 1967, after five years of planning. One thousand invitations sent to executives and community and business leaders announced a preview dinner and tour of the new store on March 3. The following Friday evening, a student body officers' fashion show and tours through the teen departments introduced young people to the store.

During this same period Bennett orchestrated a complicated plan for the expansion of the company, including projections for a 100,000–square-foot store in Granger at the

119

Valley Fair Mall in July 1970 and a 160,000–square-foot store in Orem. Possible locations in Idaho were given careful consideration; the plan for demolition and rebuilding of the downtown store and the upgrading of existing properties continued on course. Support of expansion projects was far from unanimous among board members, although Bennett would later recognize the support of Church president David O. McKay: "He had the great breadth of vision. For years to come, we shall reap the benefit of his faith in the future and of his courage to move into it with vigor as important company projects are completed — projects to which he gave his earnest consideration and wholehearted approval."[3]

Some of the board's fears were put to rest when with the addition of the Cottonwood and Ogden stores actual realized profits far exceeded pro forma projections of business. This increased the likelihood that similar projects would gain support in the future.

A comparison of ZCMI's sales to the gross national product during this important decade of expansion and change illustrated the strength of the company's position. Between 1960 and 1970 the GNP of the United States rose from $503.7 billion to $971.1, an increase of 93 percent. Sales at ZCMI during the same time period rose from $14,786,000 to $35,000,000, an increase of 137 percent.

In 1968 ZCMI was a company with a one-hundred-year history of steady growth. Its roots ran deep and wide through the community, held strong by traditional loyalties and a respected reputation for fair business practices.

Plans for a centennial celebration began early in 1967 with support from every department in the company — ZCMI's one-hundredth birthday would be ushered in with style. Designers set to work on special shopping bags, boxes, gift wrap, stationery, and even tourist postcards to commemorate the event. A unified look pulled the entire store into the effort.

October 15, 1968, was the kickoff day of ZCMI's centennial celebration. Throughout the day management met with employees at the various stores to present each a portrait of Brigham Young and to award twenty-five shares of ZCMI stock to the lucky winner of an in-house drawing. At noon a magnificent birthday cake that stood five feet six inches high was carefully cut by children lucky enough to have their birthdays on that day.

Fortunately, October 15 was a warm fall day; the festivities continued long into the evening hours. Utah's Newspaper Agency Corporation hosted an extravagant black-tie dinner at the Salt Lake Country Club. There a select gathering of about seventy guests — business, civic, and Church leaders — sampled cakes formed in the image of ZCMI and viewed a presentation of "A Store is Born," detailing the organization of the company. The rest of the employees gathered later that week at the Valley Music Hall to celebrate the beginning of a new era with music by BYU's "Sounds of Freedom." The finale was a community sing of the "ZCMI Centennial Song" to the melody of the "Battle Hymn of the Republic."

The centennial celebration continued for several months after its October beginning and became a community event as well. Weekly ads in local newspapers, radio, and television heralded "Great Moments in Utah and ZCMI's history," trying to communicate the enthusiasm felt by management for the company's proud history.

Perhaps the most enjoyed centennial project was the series of old-time shop fronts built along the South Temple facade of the store. Windows converted into shops mirrored the architecture of the early combination of member stores that ran up and down Main Street in the 1870s. Young women in puffed-sleeve, Victorian, candy-colored plaid dresses cheerfully marketed warm bread dripping with butter and honey, root-beer floats overflowing onto the counter of the soda fountain, ice cream treats, and gift items reminiscent of days long past.

For the centennial celebration ZCMI received one of fifteen national awards presented by the International Newspaper Advertising Executives for the best advertising ideas of 1968.[4]

The decade that began in 1962 with the opening of the Cottonwood Mall store and ended in 1972 with the opening of a branch store at the University Mall was one of unprecedented expansion. Expansion more than any other single issue stood out in company meetings; planning for the 1967 opening of the Ogden store, in 1970 the Valley Fair Store, and the intricate scheme required for the projected ZCMI Center and reconstructed downtown store dominated the agenda of all concerned with the company's operations. Between 1962 and 1972 growth was reflected in doubled sales, which moved from $20,237,000 in the first year of operation of the Cottonwood branch to $43,914,000 when ZCMI included five stores, at downtown Salt Lake City, Cottonwood, Valley Fair, Ogden, and University Mall in Orem, Utah.

Harold H. Bennett turned seventy in September of 1970. Unable to pull himself away from his work before seeing the last of his pet projects come to fruition, he had served through a series of five one-year extensions on his retirement. Bennett would work through three more, expressing his willingness to accommodate the strategy of the chairman of the board. This last year had been a profitable one for the company that had absorbed so much of his energy and interest over the past forty-seven years. Business was good at the Cottonwood and Ogden stores, as it was at the downtown store base. Data on the company's profitability showed a year of dramatic movement forward. One study showed that after-tax profits had increased by 61 percent in 1969, as compared to the 3 percent experienced by sixty-eight other department stores (including J.C. Penney and Sears.)[5] This was encouraging considering the amount of expansion the company had undertaken during the past several years.

When Bennett was hospitalized in December of 1972 with his third serious heart surgery it became obvious that this yearly change of his retirement plans had to stop. But for many Bennett epitomized the best of ZCMI – no matter who was chosen to succeed him, the transition would be difficult.

Just one month before Harold Bennett would finally retire, he saw the fruits of his long planning for a branch store of ZCMI in Orem, Utah. The new University Mall store was essentially the same size as the Cottonwood ZCMI in 1972: 163,000 square feet. Three large stories of selling space were quickly filled with the best ZCMI had to offer its customers. Each of the three levels could be reached by a glass-enclosed elevator that ran up the center of the store. A skylight filled the store interior with a soft, diffused light that filtered down to the separate levels. The building's exterior simultaneously set the store apart from the mall itself and harmoniously connected them. Glittering white-glazed brick stretched the length of the building, interrupted only by gold screens that spanned across the entrances. The opening of the Orem store was a satisfying end to Bennett's many years of service to the company.

President Harold H. Bennett's retirement was celebrated in a manner befitting his longtime and generous service to the institution. The company hosted a series of open houses, luncheons at the Alta Club as well as one at the state capitol, for those important leaders of the company and the community who had worked with him on so many different projects. An elegantly bound volume of letters from employees whose lives had been touched by his influence, in addition to a formal resolution of appreciation from the board of directors, attempted to summarize his contributions to the institution. Harold Bennett's shadow would long grace the walls of the store he had loved so much and so long, and would serve as a reminder of the importance of his work.

President Nathan Eldon Tanner of the LDS Church's First Presidency led the search committee for Bennett's successor. Tanner had a ten-year history of active involvement with ZCMI as a member of the board of directors. When Tanner joined the board he spent several months familiarizing himself with ZCMI's operations, holdings, and business methods. In the seventeen years he served on the board, six as chairman, Tanner was intimately concerned with management policy and practice. Oakley S. Evans was his hand-picked choice to replace longtime president Harold Bennett. Evans had recently celebrated his own retirement from the J.C. Penney Company and returned to work only after much persuasion on the part of Nathan Eldon Tanner.

Like the scrambling in the wake of a presidential election, Evans quickly moved to bring his own men to the executive office, shuffling around upper management like never before. Oakley S. Evans had a distinct style of management, and to make it work effectively he needed his own men.

Evans sought to match his team with his goals for the company: "When in business, you have to decide your objectives and your alternatives. No matter what area you're

Oakley S. Evans, president of ZCMI from 1973 to 1983.

talking about, the same principles apply. You make changes where they are needed. But I've found that at ZCMI I have tried to build on strengths already established."[6]

The organizational structure of the company was changed to accommodate these new personalities and assumptions about responsibilities and accountability. As the new manager of planning and development, Milo Carlston (also formerly of J.C. Penney) joined Evans in sketching plans for the further expansion of ZCMI. In 1974 Keith Mitchell was promoted from University Store manager to Manager of Stores.

Mitchell also began his career with J.C. Penney, but in 1959 left to join ZCMI.

In January 1975, a sweeping overhaul of upper management was announced that led to even greater stratification and specialization. Evans appointed John Ruppel, who had worked at J.C. Penney for ten years, as manager of the downtown store; Keith Saunders as internal auditor; he also moved Carlston to director of corporate facilities and planning. Longtime ZCMI executive Wendell Adams became vice president of personnel services, Dean R. Williams vice president of finance and secretary-treasurer of the corporation, and Joseph Anderson vice president of merchandising. Many of these positions reflected Evans's penchant for extending and maintaining his personal control over all aspects of the business.

Until his retirement from J.C. Penney, Oakley Evans had helped direct store planning and development. During that period he directed or helped direct the growth of the company from 1,200 to 1,800 stores, as well as its expansion into the European market.

Evans was the perfect man to slip into Bennett's shoes and move forward with the carefully constructed design of expansion. He did so without skipping a beat and rapidly matched Bennett's vision. When Evans joined ZCMI, plans were already in place for the new downtown store and adjoining mall, and stores in Granger; Cache Valley, Idaho; and Sandy, Utah. The idea for consolidating all offices and service and warehouse departments under one roof had recently surfaced. It would be his job to insure that those dreams materialized.

At age sixty Evans still followed a demanding schedule of 7:00 A.M. to 6:00 P.M. workdays at the same time that he was president of the Tabernacle Choir and active in the community.

For Evans, strong family life and unreserved community service were the two key elements to a healthy, prosperous society. "It is important that every person in every walk and station of life support those activities that will promote the good of the community," he said. "A community is the whole of its parts and the parts are interrelated." He pointed out the importance of having a strong cultural life and strong government founded on a well-informed, participating populace. "A person should assess his time and talent, and then direct it in the direction it will be most effective."[7]

Evans brought with him a significant expertise and fascination for merchandising that could not be matched. His unwavering expectation of excellence among those closest to the top kept all around him on their toes. "He taught me all about preparation. If you went into a meeting with Mr. Evans he expected you to be prepared," said Nancy Mortensen; "the alternative was too awful to think about." Using Truman's famous words, Evans reminded his cohorts, "The buck stops here."

One of the first items of business Evans confronted was an idea for a service center in which to consolidate all ZCMI offices and service departments. Ideally, bringing receiving and marking, packing, delivery, shipping, supply, sales promotion and display departments, warehouse, and bakery under one roof would increase efficiency and improve communication between the ever more complicated umbrella of services that ZCMI offered. When the idea was first presented to the board in December 1971, the projected cost of the center was $2,085,000.

Over the next year a more careful study set minimum

The ZCMI Service Center at 9th West and 21st South consolidated all offices and service departments.

criteria for the service center, selected a location at 9th West and 21st South, and finalized a contract with Zions Securities Corporation that allowed for a trade of the present warehouse facility as partial payment. The new building would include 343,000 square feet of office and warehouse space. The plan included access to railroad lines, an expanse of employee and visitor parking, and a location in industrial Salt Lake City, which combined to make it a convenient and efficient alternative to the more haphazard tradition of locating separate departments in places across town.

By June 1973 the idea had been expanded even further to include corporate offices as well. Traditionally, the office of the company president and his chief executives had been on the third floor of the downtown store. When the company included only one store this was an effective base from which the president could keep a handle on what was going on in the company.

But by 1973 this justification could no longer be used. A

ZCMI President Oakley S. Evans (left) and Governor Calvin L. Rampton hoist shovels at the new Service Center.

more efficient use of this space, and one that would be incorporated into the design of the new store, was for sales. During the demolition of the downtown store the executive office suite had been relocated, on a temporary basis, to space formerly occupied by the *Deseret News* at 33 South Richards Street, just a short walk west of the store. Despite the inconvenience of crossing the street and cutting through stores on the west side of Main Street, business had proceeded with remarkable efficiency.

The advantage of a total consolidation of offices promised all kinds of benefits. The lower costs of office space, only $1.25 per square foot, guaranteed a $65,000 annual savings. For most employees the new service center would actually be more accessible and parking would be free of charge. A final economic bonus was the reduction of space and rent owed to Zions Securities Corporation.

When it was completed the cost of the service center far exceeded its original projections, ending up at $7,237,826. The ribbon-cutting ceremony was on Tuesday, April 29, 1975, at 11:30 A.M., just three months before the opening of the ZCMI Center Mall.

ZCMI held its leadership position through traditional connections to the community symbolized by the facade of the flagship. When discussions for the renovation and rebuilding of the downtown store focused on the future of the cast-iron facade, the board divided almost evenly. Some favored an entirely new, modern look for the store; others, feeling more deeply the importance of preserving something of the past, supported the idea of making some effort to save it. Harold Bennett seemed to be closer in sentiment to the latter and urged the committee to explore every possible avenue. One idea, which was quickly vetoed, was to consider hanging the facade on a new South Temple entrance.

Some members of the community had similar concerns. One preservation-minded group organized to save ZCMI's famous storefront from the same plight that had been suffered by the Coalville Tabernacle. The group, led by Chair Christie Freed, used numerous creative tactics to bring this cause to media attention. Editorials, articles, letters to Bennett and other board members flooded ZCMI's offices. Freed convinced Bennett to stamp all outgoing correspondence with a slogan that read: "ZCMI's Main Street Facade is IRREPLACE-ABLE, HELP SAVE IT."

But when opinion of the board was finally swayed and they became committed to the restoration of the cast-iron facade, they threw in their full support and put their confidence in a man perfectly suited to the work. Formal announcement of the project was made in May 1973 in the *Salt Lake Tribune*:

> Sales and other income of Zion's Co-operative Mercantile Institution reached a record high for the fiscal year ending January 31, 1972, said Oakley S. Evans, president, and Harold B. Lee, chairman of the board. But net income was down because of "certain extraordinary expenses" caused in part by the rebuilding of the downtown store in Salt Lake City. Evans also announced that the historic Main Street facade would be reconstructed and developed into an arcade at the Main Street entrance. The man chosen to direct the work was local architect, Steven Baird.[8]

Steven Baird, the man who led the restoration of Mormon Nauvoo, had never tackled the incredible task of restoring a cast-iron facade. "This was the first time a cast iron facade has been restored and we had to relearn an old craft. We simply went back to the original system used and put it to the test."[9]

In the 1800s, formidable monuments formed in cast iron created a dignified front for new cities throughout the Western United States. James Bogardus developed the technique in the mid-nineteenth century as an alternative to the carved stonework that required much time and the costly employ of several craftsmen. The resulting look was much the same and more within the reach of the aggressive business community of this developing region. At the same time, cast iron lent strength to the building's structure and allowed the design of wider windows, creating a light and airy interior. Critics scoffed initially at this extraordinary change of long-held traditions in secular architecture, but it was quickly imitated and popularized throughout the country.

Baird directed the restoration project that would soon in-

Restoring the historic ZCMI facade was an artistic as well as a technical endeavor.

volve the talents of many of Utah's finest craftsmen: the Rumel Pattern Shop made wood molds, the State Brass Foundry cast new segments, and Metals Manufacturing Company assembled them. In total the project was like an immense jigsaw puzzle, but one with a hitch — one-third of the pieces were missing and the whole had to be put back into a form that was not quite understood.

The facade itself was constructed in three separate increments. Each of the three levels of neoclassical Corinthian columns had been cast at different times. "Instead of carving stone, they'd carve wood and take the pieces to a foundry. This way, a relatively few men could economically build the facades."[10] The lowest level presented the greatest challenge of all. In 1903 this level of columns had been removed to make room for display windows. It seemed the design for this section could not be duplicated with the same accuracy as the rest of the facade. When the facade was actually being pulled from the supports that connected it to the wood front of the store, remnants of three separate columns were found. This helped Baird and his research team to piece together the design of these elusive lower-level supports. "It meant having to relearn how to make a wood pattern."[11] Baird discovered that although the columns on the upper floor were rounded, "the main floor columns were square. So we've recast the main floor columns as close to the original as we can—and they are square."[12]

The north section, which had originally been added in 1891, had to be entirely recast. This part of the facade was constructed with sheet metal, formed over a wooden superstructure. Those observing the process considered the use of wood molds extremely innovative. The central and south sections were cast from the more traditional sand molds.

A second problem of monumental proportions was the enormous amount of paint—three-fourths of an inch, or twelve coats—that had to be sandblasted from the surface of the cast iron to find what kinds of screws had been used to connect the separate sections. A huge amount of paint remover along with blow torches and picks helped peel away layers and layers of paint to expose nuts and bolts. Many of the capitals that headed the columns had as many as eighteen separate components. One hundred eight different castings in a single vertical section increased the complexity of this giant puzzle. Multiplied by twenty-four such sections, the problem of reconstruction became enormous.

It took six weeks of careful, meticulous work to disassemble the facade and move the old pieces to a vacant lot. Approximately 50 percent of the original material was reusable; the rest was recast from wood patterns carved by hand. New pieces were cast in the State Foundry in aluminum—a material that was tougher, impervious to moisture, and, more important, weighed less.

Before the restored facade was put back into place a massive steel grid was erected that formed the structural background for the storefront. The facade now stands a few feet in front of the building itself. While Western Steel and Christiansen Bros. were hoisting the frame on the front of the building, one of the forty-five-foot-high, twelve-inch-square columns slipped out of the cinch and crashed into the cab of a Fetzer's Cabinet Company truck parked in front of the store.

Despite such drawbacks, the result transcended expectations and inspired at least twelve similar projects that Baird would head during that year alone. The facade's sparkling face shone even brighter than before. Smoothed over the newly cast front was an emollient composed of top-quality rust-protective enamels. A warm pale stone color formed a base over the entire surface, upon which gold leaf and white and brown detailing in a Victorian mode created a decorative and pleasing result. The intricate design of the framework was accentuated by spotlights placed immediately behind and across the street from the facade.

Work on the face of the new store was only part of the project. While the historic ZCMI facade was being restored, the demolition and reconstruction of the old store proceeded at a rapid pace. By the time of the stockholders' meeting held in May 1973 ZCMI's new president, Oakley Evans, was able to announce:

> Phase I of this project is nearing completion and in mid-1973 the selling departments will move on a temporary basis into the portion of the new store that is completed. Then the old store will be torn down, and the remainder of the new store erected on the site. It is expected that the entire structure will be completed, occupied, and open for business by early Spring 1975.[13]

134

Perhaps this was an overly optimistic prophecy, but this phased type of reconstruction did permit the store to continue business as usual. By September the move from the old building to the new quarters next door was almost complete. Special design and decor crews continued to work for a few weeks putting the finishing touches on selling areas so that the store would "be able to adequately serve our customers for the next two years."[14]

The grand opening of the new ZCMI Center Mall took place on July 17, 1975. Only two stores opened on that first day—Joseph Magnin and Weisfield Jewelers—but others soon followed. At that time only one of the three available floors of the parking terrace was in use: the fifth floor, which held 250 cars. On the arcade level through the mall elevators ZCMI had its only entrance to mall parking. The third- and fourth-floor level entrances to the parking mall were not completed until mid-August. During construction a ZCMI shuttle bus carried customers to and from a parking lot at 3rd West and 1st South.

The ten months before the grand opening of the finished downtown ZCMI were busy ones for the company. Each month or two the store opened a new section, connected by a ramp or roped-off corridor to the rest of the building. The sounds and smells of construction — sawdust, riveters, timber falling — were ever present. The first departments to reopen were in the basement of the store. In November 1975 hardware, housewares, small appliances, and toy departments, as well as the snack bar and bakery, moved to the lower level of the new building. In January the long-standing tradition of offering produce and grocery departments continued when odors of fresh vegetables and fruits spread from the corner of the same level. Two weeks later the store manager,

John Ruppel, and his staff moved into their offices on the third floor. During February the Budget Store, formerly located on the fourth floor, moved into its new quarters, making the final addition to the lower level.

Come spring, the main floor was completed and occupied in stages. Silverware, china, glassware, and fine gifts were the first to return to their traditional spots on the main floor by the Main Street entrance. Just days later, the series of men's departments — the Bailiwick, Boys, Suits, and so forth — were moved, decorated, and stocked in their new spots. Construction on the other half of the main floor came to a finish during April. (Until then, traffic moved between the two halves of the store through a temporary hall created by plywood barriers.) In the newly completed second half, accessories — handbags, cosmetics, neckware, stockings, jewelry — created a sparkling, fragrant ambiance of lush elegance.

April was the month of greatest change. After the fifteenth of the month the third floor quickly filled up with domestics, major appliances, and home-entertainment systems — televisions, stereos, and radios. The same week, construction on the fourth floor was completed. Soon ZCMI's home division spread across the fourth floor: couches, lamps, beds, tables, floor coverings, and accessories from exotic cloisonne to porcelain statuettes.

In May the second floor opened. Women could finally shop for the latest fashions in spacious elegance in the newly completed Women's Shoes, Fashions, Intimate Apparel, and the Ladder. The Cameo Room presented a costlier line of merchandise to those interested in a more exclusive look. The next month Miss ZC, the Loft, and Fashion Sportswear completed the second floor women's departments, offering a wide selection of clothes—from cotton turtlenecks in every hue to the most filmy silks—for every occasion.

During the ten years between 1962 and 1972 the company's total square footage went from 350,000 to 982,000. During the next decade ZCMI reaped the rewards of expansion when sales rose from $43,914,000 in 1972 to $141,263,000 in 1982. President Oakley Evans watched this growth and sought to direct it into even more profitable channels. "Aggressive merchandising will build sales volume," he would say. An aggressive and sweeping merchandise program was for Oakley Evans the key to his administration of ZCMI.

The overall dramatic rise in retailing during the 1960s led the company to accommodate change in other ways as well as through expansion. ZCMI had always leased certain departments to specialists who could offer services and products more efficiently than the company itself. Increasingly, leasing became a popular way of solving merchandising problems because of competition and an influx of specialty stores into the state. Leased departments accounted for an increased percentage of ZCMI's total sales.

The way the Wohl Shoe Company moved in 1969 into ZCMI's shoe department as a lessee serves as a case in point. ZCMI had a long tradition of hands-on involvement in the shoe business. Its shoe factory had closed only thirty years earlier. So the decision to lease the shoe department to outsiders was painfully and laboriously debated. But those who supported the idea anticipated untold advantages to be reaped in the effort. They saw a leased shoe department as a final way to combat the formidable reputation of Auerbach's well-known and popular shoe department.

Through establishing a lease department, it was hoped, a greater share of the Utah shoe business would come to ZCMI.

ZCMI was guaranteed a 20 percent sales gain in the first year. "We could even become the leader in the shoe market," one enthusiastic proponent declared. The Wohl Shoe Company was part of a huge shoe organization, with greater awareness of new trends, faster turnover, fresher stock, and finally, with better trained personnel. Slower selling shoes could be shipped to other markets. Perhaps more important, leasing the department would reduce the company's investment yet guarantee some income. And the up-to-date, competitive line of shoes would be a draw to customers, who would then shop the rest of the store.[15]

Rather than succumb to the overwhelming competition of the specialty shop, ZCMI often chose to bring the specialist aboard and upgrade services through the lease department. ZCMI's Auto Centers were traditionally lease departments that proved a particularly easy relationship to maintain. In November 1967 Gates Rubber signed a lease agreement with the company, in which ZCMI received as rent $27,000 or 10 percent of sales, whichever was greater. The purpose of the leased department was a commitment to providing specialized services under the umbrella of ZCMI.

ZCMI after 1973 was no longer the shadow of its pioneer predecessor that it had been only ten years earlier. It was something new — progressive, expansive, modern in every way. It sold the best merchandise marketed with the latest advertising techniques to an ever more sophisticated group of customers. The organization of this newly expanded and diverse group of stores and personalities likewise needed to change. One accommodation with several branch entities was the creation of a new position: Manager of Stores. This position — first held by Keith Mitchell, who was promoted from manager of the University Mall store — was the organization hub of the system of stores that were part of ZCMI. Mitchell met with individual store managers on a regular basis, and kept close watch over the central buying organization, which also filtered through this office. Merchandise was received centrally in Salt Lake City and shipped to local stores by shuttle trucks. Advertising in local newspapers and periodicals was prepared by promotion from the central office. At least in terms of organization, ZCMI—whether in Orem, Granger, or downtown Salt Lake City—was one single entity.

Second, Evans thought that if ZCMI were to continue to grow, the company needed a center for research-oriented projects, development activities, and areas of responsibilities. The first manager of planning and development was Milo Carlston, who had earlier taken an active role in expansion.

Perhaps Evans's most popular move came during his first year, when he quickly acted to make ZCMI's remuneration system match that of other department stores across the country. This was a change long overdue and long anticipated. It had been several years since the pay scale had been updated to match inflation rates and changes in cost of living. ZCMI had paid its employees less than comparable businesses both in Utah and across the country. Evans also improved the retirement program, and again his experience at J.C. Penney helped him in this. He used the model of major department stores that more equitably provided for their faithful, long-term employees upon retirement.

Employees at ZCMI enjoyed numerous benefits during the decades between 1962 and 1982. The pension plan in existence in 1962 created a nice cushion for all employees with two or more years of experience. The company paid the full cost of the plan rather than fund it through employee deductions. These monies accumulated in a trust fund that was invested for maximum security and growth. The Christmas bonus was part of the contribution to that fund. Upon retirement, employees received payments from the trust fund itself.

But ZCMI's employees did not have to wait until they stopped working for the company to enjoy benefits. One ad in the ZCMIRROR listed the following employee benefits:

Job Security
Shopping Discount
Promotion Opportunities
Employee Cafeteria
Sickness and Disability Benefits
Unemployment Compensation
Hospitalization Insurance
Workmen's Compensation
Employee Credit Union
Funeral Leave Pay
Group Life Insurance
Jury Duty Allowances
Tuition Assistance
Social Security
Paid Vacations
Paid Holidays
Pension Policy
Paid Rest Periods
Music at Work [16]

The tradition of in-store parties, departmental socials, and intercompany competitions continued. Flushed employees at the Cottonwood store swished and sashayed at a series of square dances held in the store auditorium. Potluck buffet suppers served on tables brightened by daffodils, sprays of forsythia, or colored crepe-paper streamers satisfied the hungry dancers after a long evening of fun.

Store manager Joseph Anderson took the leading role in "The Night Before the May Sale," a skit at the employee promotional for the spring white goods sale, good-naturedly donning a striped stocking cap and white nightdress for the part.

The store closed at 3:00 P.M. on the summer day of the traditional employees' Lagoon Day, which continued down through the 1970s. Perhaps the inevitable result of the wide expansion of the company and the subsequent rise in number of employees was that this type of activity increasingly was held on a local, in-house basis rather than as a gathering of the entire company.

Evans was the first to admit that ZCMI was only as strong as its employees. Fashion strategy was impossible without a fine team of buyers and sales associates who, after all, made the ultimate contact with customers.

In one issue of the ZCMIRROR a few salesclerks remembered their most satisfying sales experiences. Carol Davis, from Cottonwood Toys, recalled a young mother whose only son was mentally retarded but gifted, in her mind, creatively. The mother would comb the shelves of the toy department searching for "Paint By Number" sets for the little boy, returning on occasion to show Mrs. Davis his progress.

Corrine King exemplified the best type of salesmanship when she assisted a woman who came into ZCMI on her eighty-seventh birthday. The woman carefully walked into the dress department leaning on her cane. She purchased a warm blue knit dress and, "although physically and mentally alert, she expressed a desire to have a steady hand on her arm as she shopped for a matching hat in the millinery department." Mrs. King went with her to the glove display, choosing an appropriate pair of gloves to top off the look. But the woman wasn't quite finished yet. She took her sales friend with her to the shoe department for the rest of her ensemble.

Men were accomplishing much the same good in their own departments. Andy Thomson, for one, encountered a large fellow who had come down from Idaho to find a pair of trousers big enough to fit his newly enlarged frame. He had been unable to find any clothes to fit him in his hometown. Mr. Thomson so sympathetically and efficiently helped him resolve his problem that he left ZCMI with not only the trousers but four suits and a sports coat.[17]

A final and perhaps most enduring change made under Evans's direction was a greater commitment to fashion. "Fashion leadership is the focus of all our merchandising programs," he would say. We must have an "aggressive fashion strategy, 'upgrading the lifestyle' " of our customers.[18] With Evans's encouragement, increased attention was paid to the fashion dimension of ZCMI's business. In the process, ZCMI changed and became less a true department store but one more oriented toward clothing, and in particular a tradition of conservative fashion trends. In many ways, that direction matched the objectives of the company's founders. ZCMI would not market outlandish fashions or unorthodox merchandise—it was a company with a sense of who it was and who its customers were.

Interestingly enough, the report of the merchandising division supports this change as a wise financial move. The various ready-to-wear departments represented the majority of total sales. Perhaps even more important, gross margins

ZCMI sponsored numerous fashion shows under the direction of Joyce Gorder.

were significantly higher for clothing than for other types of goods sold throughout the store.

ZCMI's fashion office was led for many years by a woman whose creative energies and sense of style matched the unique tradition of ZCMI. As fashion coordinator Joyce Gorder, a former Mrs. Utah and model herself for many years, initiated countless special events to promote sales at ZCMI. Fashion shows conceived and organized by Gorder and her fashion office — whether elaborate *Vogue* magazine shows for charity luncheons or informal in-house shows with models walking through the store or the Tiffin Room — brought women into the store.

As fashion coordinator, Joyce Gorder usually arranged

from ten to fifteen such shows each year — working with every department in the store on promotion, contacting buyers for the latest products, selecting, accessorizing, numbering, and labeling each outfit. The script, lighting, music, and choreography for each show tested the creative limits of this talented woman.

Gorder's work matched the objectives of Oakley Evans and his successors, who wanted ZCMI to match competitors with the most up-to-date fashion merchandise. Gorder's contact with representatives of local high schools on ZCMI's teen board, "The Youngtimers," extended her fashion know-how throughout the community.[19]

Ron Nelson, director of visual merchandising, spent his entire career at ZCMI. Under his artistic direction, the company's window displays received first place recognition by the Visual Merchandising's International Display Competition for seven consecutive years.

The year 1976, which ushered in the country's bicentennial, was a good one for ZCMI. The downtown store and ZCMI Center Mall were finally finished; the move to the service center was complete. Pre-opening expenses and half-year occupancy costs of the two new stores were largely absorbed by sales increases. In July ZCMI opened a 61,000–square-foot store at Logan, Utah, which brought the company back to Cache Valley after seventy-four years.

The value of ZCMI stock remained remarkably constant over the years. Changes in valuation reflected outside pressures: depression, recession, war; or inside changes: expansion, changed buying policies, growth, or stock splits. Dividends paid on stocks varied from as high as $12.00 paid in the early twentieth century to less than $1.00 during the decade of the greatest expansion between 1962 and 1972.

Despite a 300 percent stock dividend in 1917 and 100 percent stock dividends in 1956 and again in 1978, dividends paid on ZCMI stock were relatively conservative, never dropping inordinately low or rising too high.

In 1964 the board changed the par value of ZCMI stock from $50 to $20 with a total capitalization of $7,200,000. Effective May 20, 1981, a final move in the par value of ZCMI capital stock changed 1,200,000 shares of $20 par value to 5,000,000 shares with no par value. The board authorized a three-for-one stock split effective August 25, 1983. The split was effected in the form of a 200 percent stock dividend.

The largest dip in the number of stockholders occurred between 1868 and 1889, when investors in ZCMI went from 1,000 to 528. This huge decrease can possibly be explained by the organization of local cooperatives, which for a while soaked up the capital of Utah Mormons. Between 1962 and 1982 the number of stockholders continued to increase, from 1,374 in 1962 to 1,862 in 1982. After May 1975 stock was traded over-the-counter in Salt Lake City.

Compared to many other retail institutions ZCMI was in an enviable financial position. On the national average, business for retail stores had improved by 22 percent during 1975–76, which represented about 13.3 percent on net worth. At ZCMI business had improved 65.8 percent or 13.6 percent on net worth. After-tax profits show this same improvement, a national average of 2.8 percent, compared to ZCMI's 4.2 percent increase.

But 1975 would also be the marking point of a dramatically changed national economy that would ultimately affect ZCMI as well. Two decades of postwar prosperity and growth came to a grinding halt in the mid-1970s when oil prices rose some

145

350 percent in one year. This boost in oil prices reverberated throughout the economy and soon shook the walls of ZCMI.

The company accommodated the inconveniences of the energy crisis by cooperating with fuel conservation programs, lowering store temperatures, decreasing interior and exterior lighting, and encouraging employees to set up carpools and to drive at lower speeds.

Inflation rates reflected this strain as well, jumping from 3.3 percent in 1972 to 11 percent in 1974. One way of combating the ill effects of skyrocketing inflation that affected retailers in particular was a change in the accepted method of taking inventory. In May 1975, Evans assigned Keith Saunders, the new internal auditor, to calculate the LIFO inventory adjustment. LIFO was designed to eliminate the effects of inflation and result in a substantial savings in taxes.

> In order not to overstate reported profits as a result of inflation during the year, the company changed its method of accounting for inventory from first- in, first-out to LIFO (last in first out). This was desirable because of the rapid increase in prices in 1974 which caused inventories sold to be replaced at substantially higher prices.[20]

In the first year the increase of $747,000 in cost of goods reduced taxes by $371,000 or $1.12 a share.

Despite this type of measure to strengthen ZCMI's financial position, the recession would grow in intensity and continue to plague the company. Unlike earlier fluctuations in the economy, which faded away like a summer sun's last heat, this one did not. It would spread its poison through cracks in the foundations of some of the country's oldest businesses.

Another spur to inflation was easy credit buying. Still recoiling from the postwar scarcity of goods, many people lived a perpetual buying spree. Household and business borrowing more than tripled during the mid-1970s. Credit cards made a greater variety of goods accessible to a greater number of customers. Quite simply, more people were buying what they could not afford. At the same time, this explosion in credit buying helped force up the price of everything.

By 1980 the nation was in a full-fledged recession, with unemployment of 7.5 percent. The nature of the merchandising sector would never be the same.

In 1982 ZCMI's management met an entirely different set of challenges from those of earlier generations. New pressures on gross margins and escalating operating costs prevented retailers from maintaining profit margins comparable to those of earlier years. The players were involved in a new game with a bewilderingly complex set of rules.

The deepening recession was a constant cloud over projections for future sales and improvements. The persistently high interest rate dropped from 21.5 percent in 1981 to 14 percent in 1982, but was still a constant blight on the economy. These figures were felt at ZCMI through slower sales, flat profit margins, and slower payoff of accounts receivable. Capital expenditures were needed to open new stores and to complete the modernization and expansion plans for the older ones, which were always in some state of deterioration.

Upon the retirement of President Oakley S. Evans in September 1983, Joseph Anderson, former executive vice president and longtime employee of the store, inherited the balancing act of uniting the branch stores and at the same time finding a way to let the company work within the confines of the economy.

When he became president Mr. Anderson was surrounded by a group of men who had many years of experience with ZCMI. The skeletal organization of the company revolved around the central figure of the president. Rather than ap-

Joseph A. Anderson, president of ZCMI from 1983 to 1985.

point managers of the separate divisions, the company made a number of vice presidents responsible and accountable for its diverse aspects. In 1983 Milo Carlston was vice president of development; Lowell M. Durham Jr., who had joined the company in January of that year, was vice president of stores; John Ruppel, vice president of sales and merchandising; and Keith Saunders was vice president of finances as well as corporate secretary-treasurer.

The board of directors represented, similarly, a diversity of expertise and long history of traditional association with the company. Chair Marvin J. Ashton, apostle of The Church of Jesus Christ of Latter-day Saints and a warm, kind-hearted man, was the virtual leader of the company. His intelligent and intuitive business sense would be reflected in both leadership and policy of ZCMI during these years. In addition to Elder Ashton and store president Joseph Anderson, the board included attorney Stephen Anderson, local businessmen Dan Bushnell and Allan Hunter, banker Spencer Eccles, Patricia Madsen (a descendant of Richard W. Madsen), apostle L. Tom Perry, and Keith Saunders. One hundred and twenty years after the board first met, the traditional combination of ecclesiastical and business leaders continued. Board and company executives divided into three committees to deal with certain issues they were best suited to discuss. The audit, retirement, and executive committees met independent of the board and formed policies, made reports, and did studies.

As president, Joseph Anderson saw sales increase in 1983 by 5.3 percent and in 1984 by 6.9 percent. When he retired in 1985 after thirty-six years with the company and became vice chair of the board of directors, he was described in the 1985 Report to Stockholders as a man who "epitomized the company's ideals of loyalty, service and achievement." Joseph Anderson held the reins of ZCMI management during a period when retailers nationwide faced considerable challenges.

When Anderson became president in 1983 the plans were in place for stores at the Layton Hills Mall (April 1980), Pine Ridge Mall, Chubbuck, Idaho (July 1981), and Grand Teton Mall, Idaho Falls, Idaho (August 1984). Each of these new stores would be substantially smaller than normal. These smaller stores did not carry the full line of goods and services available at the larger branches of ZCMI.

Stores like the Downtown or Cottonwood branches had a different agenda to fulfill. Merchandising there considered "the customer who is more fashion, quality, value con-

A skyway connects the Ogden ZCMI store with the Ogden Mall across the street.

scious."[21] The new and often formidable competition presented by Nordstrom, Mervyn's, and other newcomers to the Salt Lake retail scene inspired change.

Never before had so much retail space been added in the ZCMI market areas as during the past year and a half. The result was an oversaturated retail market that would take several years to be brought back into balance. This fact, the recession, and the accompanying tightening of money sources slowed down considerably plans for future stores in Sandy and in Idaho. The tremendous expansion of the past two decades moved cautiously to a gradual denouement brought about by extraordinary conditions in the economy at large and the need for renewed attention to the central organization.

Between 1973 and 1983, when the number of stores went from five to eight, the number of employees jumped dramatically. In 1973 ZCMI had 1,920 workers in its separate locations. By 1983 that figure had swelled to include the equivalent of 2,429 full-time employees and possibly another

1,000 part-time individuals working in the company's eight stores and the service center. It was no longer possible for the store president to know even the names of all his employees, let alone something about them. Logistically the problems of administration of such a large and unwieldy company had blown to new proportions. The feeling of family that had been such an important part of the store in the 1930s and 40s was diffused and for many lost in the process.

Lowell M. Durham Jr. was the impetus behind a new program of employee compensation and accountability that attempted to create a more equitable basis for sales personnel and to make more tangible the links between employees and the business of the store. "Commitment to Excellence" was a sweeping program of change in employee procedures and policies. Customer service was given new attention. Salesclerks were from that point known as "associates," joining them to the important work of management and the overall success of the company. Sales associates were encouraged to improve their own personal appearance through the best hygiene and fashion. They were told to know their merchandise, not just camp out at the cash register, but be an active, vital feature of the selling floor, offering advice when needed, being a helpful, ever-present representative of the fashion office. In addition to improving personal appearance, polishing selling skills, and gaining information about merchandise, the associate needed to understand personnel goals and systems of compensation, which varied from department to department. Durham established a commission system where appropriate in new departments throughout the store.

The "Commitment to Excellence" program was piloted at the University Mall store and because of its success there was soon installed in all stores. The result was overwhelmingly positive, as reflected in significantly improved morale among employees who took an active part in the program, who felt in a new way a part of the company.

In 1985 the employee "Commitment to Excellence" program would be followed by a customer program called "Extras Make Excellence." Again the brainchild of Lowell M. Durham Jr., this new customer-service program reflected the original objectives of the store's founders of keeping customers happy through fair prices, decent trade policies, and extras.

This commitment to service would occasionally involve great cost to the company but would be unwavering during the next three years. Four basic "extras" helped make shopping at ZCMI an attractive alternative to the competition. First, the company's return policy insured that if customers were not satisfied with their purchases, for whatever reason, they could return them for a full refund, credit, or exchange. Although it took many of the older salesclerks a while to adjust to this change (they often acted as if it were money out of their own pockets), the policy soon became standard throughout the store. The second policy was easily as popular and again reflected the traditional goal of maintaining fair prices. If a customer came into ZCMI and said, "This jacket is on sale across the street," the item would be sold for the exact same price at ZCMI. Price matching was again often done at a loss for the company, but expressed an unwavering willingness to do all possible to be competitive in the marketplace and give good values. ZCMI was one of the last big companies to offer free gift wrap (at an annual cost of $1,700,000). The "Personal Shopper" would help customers find just the right gift at a moment's notice, or help make fashion choices for the less confident buyer. The Wedding

Registry simplified shopping for presents for new brides, insuring just the right choices. Customer comments on these and other improvements, complaints, and ideas for new extras filtered through a newly created committee called the Customer Service Advisory Board, which met quarterly to form a conduit between management and the customer.

Excellent customer service went far beyond the contact between customer and sales associate. At ZCMI customer service continued behind the scenes. ZCMI offered credit programs that made it possible for anyone to finance large purchases. Besides accepting all major third-party credit cards, ZCMI offered a charge card that opened one of four credit plans. First was the option plan, where the customer was billed 10 percent of the balance; second, the club plan for purchasing sets of china or silver was interest free for up to two years; third, special sales offered twelve months of interest-free credit; and finally, vendor-sponsored promotional sales offered a similar twelve-month interest-free account. A twenty-four-month time-payment plan was always available.

These programs were typical of the way Lowell M. Durham Jr. worked after 1985 as president of ZCMI. He encouraged a new respect for how people felt about what they were doing, and set up a system of ad-hoc committees to involve experts from all across the store in the decision-making process. Durham's management style centered in a system of accountability that allowed a remarkable amount of autonomy among his colleagues in the executive office. After he had delegated responsibility for something he assumed that it would be done. Although ultimately answerable for the success or failure of all company programs or policies, Durham felt comfortable in that role. On a local radio program

Lowell M. Durham Jr., president of ZCMI from 1985 to 1990.

aired in November 1988 he was asked, "Isn't there an enormous amount of pressure knowing that if something goes wrong at ZCMI you will have to take the heat?" He quietly chuckled, but then said confidently, "It is, but I believe in the people around me. I know they will perform, they are a talented, bright group of men and women who understand the importance of staying power."

Perhaps Lowell M. Durham Jr.'s greatest contribution to ZCMI was making Nancy Mortensen vice president of marketing services. When Durham came to ZCMI, Mortensen was director of ZCMI's special affairs office, which headed up a grab bag of original events: the traditional fashion shows,

154

the annual ZCMI Women's Fun Run, charity events — general projects that made the public notice ZCMI. He, like Oakley Evans, recognized in her executive potential and made her the first female executive of Utah's largest department store. Perhaps equally noteworthy was that Nancy Mortensen was not only a woman but a non-Mormon. Mortensen was a significant addition to ZCMI's executive team. She lent a sophistication, an awareness of the national fashion scene that had been lacking before. As vice president of marketing services she continued to oversee special affairs and promotions. ZCMI day at Hogle Zoo, the Salute to Italy, and the Countryside of Britain promotions were enjoyed by customers and employees alike.

Durham's management team was for the most part young, bright, and ready to take on the challenge of the future. In addition to Mortensen, Keith C. Saunders added many years' experience at ZCMI in his new role as executive vice president and chief financial officer, corporate secretary-treasurer. R. Barry Arnold as vice president and general merchandise manager adeptly coordinated merchandising concerns throughout the company.

Lowell M. Durham Jr. was used to dealing with the results of radical change. For many, the choice of Durham for president of ZCMI was a controversial one. He came to ZCMI after a distinguished career in publishing as president of Deseret Book, but had little experience in department store merchandising. Mr. Durham was a quiet man, a Ph.D. in English and, like Harold H. Bennett, a national ranking squash player, perhaps more intuitively a poet than a businessman. With him the language of business took on a new metaphorical twist as he used stories and poetry to emphasize his concept of business management. Durham was hand-picked for the job by Chairman of the Board Marvin J. Ashton, who recognized in him a great talent for working with and motivating people. He knew Durham was just what ZCMI needed. One of the most difficult tasks brought to him during the first eighteen months as president was to streamline ZCMI's management team for increased efficiency and productivity.

In a series of roles as vice president of corporate development, personnel, and public relations, and finally as executive vice president, Durham saw every dimension of the business and was a quick study. One colleague would remark that as president he would in fact make a contribution to merchandising unmatched in recent years.

Answering for another sweeping change fell to Durham—the decision to discontinue the Budget Store. In 1986 ZCMI was one of the only stores in the country that maintained a budget store. This created enormous difficulties for internal buyers and strained the relationship with the central buying office. At the same time, the Budget Store was operating at a loss, each year moving deeper into a chasm caused by skyrocketing operating costs and reduced gross margins. Increased competition made competitive prices more difficult to reach. The decision to eliminate this traditional department was thoughtfully studied and executed—reflecting the internal and external pressures to change.

During the second half of the 1980s store management would struggle to adapt to what had proven to be overexpansion of the 1970s and 80s. Despite the modest success of stores in outlying areas and the favorable position each played in the life of the community, gross margins simply could not support the huge square footage that had been built. It was doubtful in 1988 that business would ever match the size of some of these branch stores.

One of the chief tasks set before Lowell M. Durham Jr. was to help a company grown too large in terms of square footage match once more the rhythm of the center by refining the organization to reflect the phenomenal growth of the two preceding decades.

The study of Zion's Cooperative Mercantile Institution is a story of the continuing interplay between tradition and change. Only by viewing this relationship over time has the subtlety and significance of this dynamic been able to emerge.

This story portrays the struggle of men (and finally women) to preserve the essential meaning at the center of this unique business. They would all undoubtedly agree that ZCMI was more than just another business. It was a business with a difference.

That illusive difference is as much as anything the story of this book, for there are issues that have persisted through this 120–year history to form the center of this company.

Business at ZCMI, like the shifting gears of a motor at the base of a gigantic factory, surged forward with a consistency and predictability that seemed to give it a life of its own. The never-failing solidity of its center, of its organization, made it a constant strength in the life of the community.

In the 1980s one board member, Spencer Eccles, suggested that ZCMI functioned as a bellwether of the economic life of the community. As was true in the nineteenth century, when business was good at ZCMI, business was generally good. The reverse was also generally true. Business at ZCMI was little affected by the caprices of men but moved forward, again with the same constancy, the same predictability, through successive changes in leadership.

157

As Utah's fifth-largest employer, ZCMI had a hold on the community that was more than traditional. It was the very lifeblood of the employees who contributed to the diverse services and products that the company provided. ZCMI's success or failure exerted a very real effect on the economic life of the state.

ZCMI would continue to reflect the shadow of its leaders. Brigham Young's prophetic hopes for the institution—fair price codes, high standards of merchandise, a commitment to service—would become a sort of gospel for succeeding generations of company executives.

The men who led the company as president were not a series of interchangeable parts. Each cast instead his own unique shadow across this institution in a way that reflected his own colors, his own vision of how to make ZCMI match the objectives of its founders.

Despite the fact that in 1980 ZCMI was a publicly held corporation with stock traded over-the-counter, it was still in a very real and intimate way connected to The Church of Jesus Christ of Latter-day Saints. The executive committee of the board of directors—as in earlier years the actual center of company power—was dominated by Church apostles and leaders, men with ecclesiastical and political power who determined the direction the company would grow.

It seemed to many that ZCMI was one of the last stores to retain a Sunday closing policy. This and the store's commitment to conservative merchandising standards again in a very real way reflect back to the traditional connection with the Church. ZCMI consciously sets a standard in the retail community for excellence and has always had a reputation for its fair treatment of customers and employees alike.

Finally, this strong and pervasive sense of history—of the

importance of this tradition—helps define this "illusive difference" that sets ZCMI apart from the rest. For in a time when chain stores come and go as quickly as hemlines move from knee to floor, ZCMI has been a company that has endured, that is a constant feature of the community, that sets standards, that has weathered many storms and has risen and continues to rise to the challenges and come out on top.

NOTES

1. ZCMIRROR, March 1962.
2. Report of Management, May 31, 1960.
3. Report of the Board of Directors, Vol. I, November 25, 1969.
4. *Salt Lake Tribune*, May 20, 1969.
5. Report of Management, August 25, 1970.
6. *California Apparel News*, August 27, 1976.
7. *Salt Lake Tribune*, May 17, 1973.
8. Ibid.
9. *Utah Holiday*, July 1976, p. 47.
10. *Salt Lake Tribune*, May 9, 1976.
11. *Deseret News*, June 12, 1976.
12. *Deseret News*, August 22, 1975.
13. *Deseret News*, May 22, 1973.
14. *Deseret News*, September 25, 1973.
15. Report of the Board of Directors, Vol. I, November 25, 1969.
16. ZCMIRROR, May 1962.
17. Ibid.
18. *California Apparel News*, August 27, 1976.
19. ZCMIRROR, June 1963.
20. Report of the Board of Directors, Vol. H, May 27, 1975.
21. Report of the Board of Directors, Vol. I, May 18, 1983.

ZCMI

INTO THE FUTURE
1986–1991

UNPRECEDENTED EXPANSION marked the decade of the 1980s for ZCMI. On July 31, 1986, ZCMI opened its tenth store, its fourth in the Salt Lake Valley, this time in Sandy, Utah. The South Towne Center Mall store brought ZCMI to an area of the valley that boasted Utah's highest income per household, and the nation's youngest population. The idea for a store in the southern end of the valley, first discussed during Harold Bennett's final years as president, materialized after nearly a decade of anticipation. The striking interior design and innovative merchandise-display concepts – mirrors, brass, and boldly simple shapes – produced a 200,000–square-foot store very much on the cutting edge of merchandising standards. The opening of the South Towne store fulfilled management's expectations and contributed to the

160

company's near 11.8 percent sales increase for 1986, which brought sales and other income to a total of $184,259,332.

Also that year, in addition to opening the South Towne store, ZCMI completed major renovation projects at the Salt Lake Downtown store and at Cottonwood, University Mall, and the Service Center. The company continued its renovation by upgrading the Valley Fair store the next year.

The year 1987 proved to be the most difficult and challenging one of the 1980s. A sluggish and stagnant national economy compounded problems felt internally by ZCMI. Under the direction of store president Lowell M. Durham Jr., ZCMI made four difficult changes in policy and concept. The decision to close the Family Store Division (the Budget Store), easily the most far-reaching change, allowed the company to focus on a more in-depth, vertical approach to merchandising. This move undoubtedly explained in part the dip in sales and profits. Second, ZCMI prepared for and executed a plan to track inventory by store. This costly and difficult change insured more precise inventory control and merchandising in the future.

In May 1987 ZCMI reacquired the failing Decorative Home lease department. Although not a planned reacquisition, the Home department rejoined ZCMI with a minimum amount of distress on the company.

Finally, ZCMI management cut approximately 7 percent of the projected 1988 expense budget. Management designed this restrictive measure to keep the company financially sound and forward looking.

That same year the company developed a Mission Statement clearly reflecting a concern for excellence in customer service, employee relations, and growth.

ZCMI MISSION STATEMENT

I. ZCMI will strive to treat its customers in an honest manner, while providing quality merchandise at a fair price. ZCMI will back this promise with outstanding service and a promise to match price fairly at any time and to accept valid returns without question. In addition, ZCMI, "America's First Department Store," feels a responsibility to support communities in which we do business. The tradition and history of ZCMI puts our place in the community as a top priority. ZCMI will strive to build and support our communities in every possible way.

II. ZCMI is committed to its employees and will treat them fairly, give them a sense of accountability, and compensate them for work performed. In addition, ZCMI will provide a sound program of benefits.

III. ZCMI will be attentive to its stockholders and strive in every way to provide a meaningful return to its owners. This return would not only come as a responsible dividend and growth in stock value, but also in seeing ZCMI remain the dominant department store in our market area and a highly respected business in every community that ZCMI serves.

IV. ZCMI will continue to plan for growth by carefully assessing the markets that ZCMI can best serve while at the same time providing ZCMI with the best opportunities for responsible growth. ZCMI is committed to growing.

V. ZCMI is committed to sound financial practices that will support the overall goals of the company. ZCMI is committed to provide a strong balance sheet to establish the basis for future growth, and to maintain the liquidity of the company to sustain current operations. In addition, ZCMI has a viable and specific five-year plan that is updated yearly and is used as a guide for planning the future.[1]

During 1988 two special concept stores at the Fashion Place Mall and at Foothill Village kicked off another year of major expansion. Management had refined this concept for a scaled-down yet more upscale fashion specialty store—ZCMI II— during 1987. With two new ZCMI II stores the company made an unprecedented move into the fashion specialty store market. The public responded so favorably to the ZCMI II concept

The ZCMI II store at Foothill Village was an immediate success.

that management began planning a third ZCMI II location. In late 1988, the company had eleven other markets into which it seriously considered expanding, including: (1) Twin Falls, Idaho; (2) St. George, Utah (where a full-line department store was opened in fall 1990); (3) Boise, Idaho; (4) Las Vegas, Nevada; (5) Mesa, Arizona; (6) Reno, Nevada; (7) Flagstaff, Arizona; (8) Prescott, Arizona; (9) Nampa, Idaho; (10) Lewiston, Idaho; and (11) Grand Junction, Colorado. Not all of the new locations would necessarily have ZCMI II stores, but many would. By the end of 1988 ZCMI included thirteen stores in seven cities and well over 1.5 million square feet of selling space.

The company's Five-Year Strategic Plan included growth

ZCMI II stores specialize in the latest fashion trends.

other than that manifested in the form of new stores. Those changes included an updated warehouse, modernized data processing and POS capabilities, continued expense control, personnel development, and market research. The Report to Stockholders in 1988 emphasized the company's long-term commitment to maintaining a tradition of excellence. Chairman of the Board Marvin J. Ashton wrote: "ZCMI is a company whose owners, employees and management have been visionary enough to see the long-term benefits of staying power. They have accepted the vision of sustained growth and stability rather than the quick profit. This is high praise for ZCMI and good news for the communities we serve."[2]

A second important part of the company's plan to improve profitability and adapt to the future included existing ZCMI facilities. Besides updating the lover level to cater more directly to downtown businesspeople, the downtown store underwent modifications to make selling space more cost effective. "Salt Lake Downstairs" included a food court and valet parking.

Lowell M. Durham Jr. resigned from ZCMI in January 1990, after seven years of service to the company. In those few years, ZCMI had added four new stores, including the two new ZCMI II stores (a downsizing concept developed by Durham), and had plans for six new stores to be opened later that year.

Durham's successor would be Richard H. Madsen, who, nearly sixty years after his grandfather Richard W. Madsen became president of ZCMI, took the reigns of the company to usher in a new decade. The Madsen family represented what one ZCMI publication called "Generations of Dedication" to ZCMI, a connection that spanned half of the 122 years of the company's history. It began with Richard W. Madsen, who led ZCMI from 1932 to 1946.

Richard W. Madsen died two years after his retirement in 1946. But his legacy of dedication and service to the company continued through his son Richard W. Madsen Jr., who succeeded his father as director. Between 1952 and 1976 Richard W. Madsen Jr. served as a member of the executive committee of ZCMI's board of directors. His daughter Patricia Madsen replaced him after his retirement from the board in 1976. Patricia H. Madsen also served on the executive committee.

Richard H. Madsen, president of ZCMI beginning in 1990.

When Richard H. Madsen became president of ZCMI the company had truly come full circle.

Richard H. Madsen, like his grandfather, brought to the helm of ZCMI wisdom and business acumen gained through an already full career in business. Former president of Madsen Furniture Galleries, Richard, son of R.W.'s son Francis Armstrong Madsen, was raised and educated in Salt Lake City. After obtaining a bachelor of science degree in marketing, he received a law degree from the University of Utah. A diversified career prepared him for the challenge of leading Utah's largest department store, and the state's fourth largest employer (with 4,500 employees). After serving two tours of active duty in the United States Army in California and Missouri, Richard H. Madsen worked from 1966 to 1967 as a law clerk to United States District Court Judge A. Sherman Christensen. The father of ten children, a lawyer, and a manager, Richard H. Madsen also taught at the University of Utah as an adjunct professor at the Graduate School of Business and College of Business. As a member of the executive committee of ZCMI's board of directors, Richard H. Madsen knew the challenges facing the store in the 1990s. Not nearly the size of his grandfather, whose physical presence was so imposing, Richard H. Madsen cut a very different figure as he walked through the stores familiarizing himself with both the personalities and products of ZCMI. But good humor and a sincere concern for the store and its employees identified both men and continued a Madsen tradition of excellence. Madsen moved gracefully from the position of president of an intimate, family owned and operated business to the very public presidency of one of the West's largest department-store chains. By the May 10 stockholders' meeting Madsen had grasped the vision of ZCMI's strategic plan for the immediate future. He detailed this plan for stockholders by emphasizing a new "reduced promotion-type" marketing approach.[3] The company's strength would be, Madsen explained, to strengthen its fashion assortment and style and deemphasize "this enormously promotional climate we're in. . . . Retailing [or] effective retailing is theatre and drama, and not necessarily sale, sale, price, price."[4]

In 1991 ZCMI looked to the future with a sense of the past

and the importance of tradition, but with excitement for a new decade of unprecedented expansion and growth. The company prepared to meet the challenges of this new decade with a new president, with sound strategies designed to generate more business and increase gross margins, and with a fresh commitment to state-of-the-art merchandising technologies. In part because of its 120–year history in the community, many consumers mistakenly confused the company with what President Richard Madsen called "a kind old dame . . . an elderly aunt of dignified bearing," an image management was determined to overturn. Whether or not they succeed will be part of another generation's chapter in ZCMI's history, yet untold.

NOTES

1. Report to Stockholders, 1987.
2. Report to Stockholders, 1988.
3. *Salt Lake Tribune,* May 16, 1990.
4. Ibid.

APPENDIX A

DIVIDENDS ON ZCMI STOCK

Year	Dividend
1878	$5.50
1879	$7.50
1880	$7.00
1881	$7.00
1882	$10.00
1883	$10.00
1884	$10.00
1885	$10.00
1886	$10.00
1887	$10.00
1888	$10.00
1889	$10.00
1890	$11.00
1891	$12.00
1892	$12.00
1893	$11.00
1894	$8.00
1895	$8.00
1896	$8.00
1897	$8.00
1898	$8.00
1899	$8.00
1900	$9.00
1901	$9.00
1902	$12.00
1903	$12.00
1904	$12.00
1905	$12.00
1906	$12.00
1907	$12.00
1908	$12.00

(3/1/09: Forty years since opening, sales aggregated $130,000,000. Cash dividend paid 37 percent.)

1909	$12.00
1910	$12.00
1911	$15.00
1912	$20.00
1913	$20.00
1914	$20.00
1915	$20.00
1916	$20.00
1917	$20.00

(300% stock dividend paid in 1917)

1918	$8.00
1919	$8.00
1920	$8.00
1921	$7.50
1922	$6.00
1923	$6.00
1924	$6.00
1925	$6.00
1926	$6.00
1927	$6.00
1928	$6.00
1929	$4.00
1930	$3.00
1931	none
1932	none

(12/27/32 — par value changed to $50)

1933		none
1934		none
1935		$2.00
1936		$3.75
1937		$2.50
1938	5 dividends at $.25 each	$1.25
1939	4 dividends at $.25 each	$1.00
1940	4 dividends at $.50 each	$2.00
1941	4 dividends at $.50 each	$2.00
1942	5 dividends at $.50 each	$2.50
1943	6 dividends at $.50 each	$3.00
1944	5 dividends, 1 at $1.00, 4 at $.75	$4.00
1945	4 dividends at $.75 each	$3.00
1946	5 dividends, 1 at $1.00; 4 at $.75	$4.00

1947- - - - - - - - - - 5 dividends, 1 at $1.00; 4 at $.75 - - - - - - - - - - - $4.00
1948- - - - - - - - - - 5 dividends, 1 at $1.00; 4 at $.75 - - - - - - - - - - - $4.00
1949- - - - - - - - - - 5 dividends, 1 at $1.00; 4 at $.75 - - - - - - - - - - $4.00
1950- - - - - - - - - - 5 dividends, 1 at $1.00; 4 at $.75 - - - - - - - - - - - $4.00
1951- - - - - - - - - - 5 dividends, 1 at $1.00; 4 at $.75 - - - - - - - - - - - $4.00
1952- - - - - - - - - - 5 dividends, 1 at $1.00; 4 at $.75 - - - - - - - - - - $4.00
1953- - - - - - - - - - 5 dividends, 1 at $1.00; 4 at $.75 - - - - - - - - - - $4.00
1954- - - - - - - - - - - - - 4 dividends at $.75 each - - - - - - - - - - - - - $3.00
1955- - - - - - - - - - - - - 4 dividends at $.75 each - - - - - - - - - - - - - $3.00
1956- - - - - - - - - - - - - - - (On 117,434 shares) - - - - - - - - - - - - - - -$1.875
      (6/15/56: 100% dividend)
1957- - - - - - - - - - -5 dividends, 4 at $.40, 1 at $.30- - - - - - - - - - - $1.90
1958- - - - - - - - - - -5 dividends, 4 at $.40, 1 at $.30- - - - - - - - - - - $1.90
1959- - - - - - - - - - -5 dividends, 4 at $.40, 1 at $.30- - - - - - - - - - - $1.90
1960- - - - - - - - - - -5 dividends, 4 at $.40, 1 at $.30- - - - - - - - - - - $1.90
1961- - - - - - - - - - - -5 dividends at $.40 each - - - - - - - - - - - - - $2.00
1962- - - - - - - - - - - -5 dividends at $.40 each - - - - - - - - - - - - - $2.00
1963- - - - - - - - - - - -5 dividends at $.40 each - - - - - - - - - - - - - $2.00
1964- - - - - - - - - - - -5 dividends at $.40 each - - - - - - - - - - - - - $2.00
      (1965: stock split—par value changed to $20.00)
1965- -$.6833, comparable to $.6666 in 1964
1966- - - - - - - - - - -5 dividends, 4 at $.15, 1 at $.10- - - - - - - - - - - $.70
1967- - - - - - - - - - -5 dividends, 4 at $.15, 1 at $.10- - - - - - - - - - - $.70
1968- - - - - - - - 5 dividends, 1 at $.15, 3 at $.20, 1 at $.05 - - - - - - - - $.80
1969- - - - - - - - - - - - -4 dividends at $.20 each - - - - - - - - - - - - - $.80
1970- - - - - - - - - - - - -4 dividends at $.25 each - - - - - - - - - - - - - $1.00
1971- - - - - - - - - - -4 dividends, 1 at $.25, 3 at $.35- - - - - - - - - - - $1.30
1972- - - - - - - - - - -5 dividends, 4 at $.35, 1 at $.05- - - - - - - - - - - $1.45
1973- - - - - - - - - - -5 dividends, 4 at $.35, 1 at $.05- - - - - - - - - - - $1.45
1974- - - - - - - - - - -4 dividends, 1 at $.35, 3 at $.40- - - - - - - - - - - $1.55
1975- - - - - - - - - - - -4 dividends at $.60 each - - - - - - - - - - - - - $1.60
1976- - - - - - - - - - -4 dividends, 1 at $.40, 3 at $.45- - - - - - - - - - - $1.75
1977- - - - - - - - - - -4 dividends, 1 at $.45, 3 at $.50- - - - - - - - - - - $1.95
1978- - - - - - - - - - -2 dividends, 1 at $.50, 1 at $.60- - - - - - - - - - - $1.10
      (6/23/78: 100% stock dividend, equivalent to $1.15 cash dividend)
1979- - - - - - - - - - - - -4 dividends at $.30 each - - - - - - - - - - - - - $1.20
1980- - - - - - - - - - -4 dividends, 1 at $.30, 3 at $.35- - - - - - - - - - - $1.35
1981- - - - - - - - - - - -4 dividends at $.35 each - - - - - - - - - - - - - $1.40
1982- - - - - - - - 4 dividends, 1 at $.34, 1 at $.35, 2 at $.38 - - - - - - - - $1.45
1983- - - - - - - - 4 dividends, 2 at $.38, 1 at $.45, 1 at $.15 - - - - - - - - $1.38

(8/25/83: 3 for 1 stock split)

1984 - - - - - - - - - - - - - -4 dividends at $.15 each - - - - - - - - - - - - - $.60
1985 - - - - - - - - - - - - - -4 dividends at $.15 each - - - - - - - - - - - - - $.60
1986 - - - - - - - - - - - - - -4 dividends at $.15 each - - - - - - - - - - - - - $.60
1987 - - - - - - - - - - - - - -4 dividends at $.15 each - - - - - - - - - - - - - $.60
1988 - - - - - - - - - - - - - -4 dividends at $.15 each - - - - - - - - - - - - - $.60
1989 - - - - - - - - - - - - - -4 dividends at $.15 each - - - - - - - - - - - - - $.60
1990 - - - - - - - - - - - - - -4 dividends at $.15 each - - - - - - - - - - - - - $.60

APPENDIX B

ZCMI OFFICERS

President	Appointment
Brigham Young	October 16, 1868–April 4, 1873
Horace S. Eldredge	April 4, 1873–October 4, 1873
Brigham Young	October 4, 1873–August 29, 1877
William H. Hooper	October 5, 1877–December 30, 1882
John Taylor	April 5, 1883–July 25, 1887
Wilford Woodruff	October 1887–September 2, 1898
Lorenzo Snow	September 15, 1898–October 10, 1901
Joseph F. Smith	October 17, 1901–November 19, 1918
Heber J. Grant	December 19, 1918–May 14, 1945
George Albert Smith	May 31, 1945–April 4, 1951
David O. McKay	April 18, 1951–April 16, 1958
Harold H. Bennett	April 16, 1958–January 23, 1973
Oakley S. Evans	February 1, 1973–August 1, 1983
Joseph A. Anderson	August 1, 1983–January 30, 1985
Lowell M. Durham, Jr.	January 30, 1985–April 1, 1990
Richard H. Madsen	April 2, 1990–

Vice President	Appointment
William H. Hooper	October 16, 1868–October 5, 1871
J. M. Bernhisel	October 5, 1871–October 4, 1873
Theodore McKean	October 4, 1873–November 10, 1875
William Jennings	November 10, 1873–May 10, 1875
Theodore McKean	June 10, 1875–October 5, 1877
William Jennings	October 5, 1877–January 15, 1886
H. S. Eldredge	January 16, 1886–September 6, 1888
Moses Thatcher	October 5, 1888–April 5, 1897
George Q. Cannon	April 5, 1897–April 12, 1901
Joseph F. Smith	May 16, 1901–October 17, 1901
George Romney	October 17, 1901–February 1, 1920

John F. Bennett (2nd VP)	May 17, 1919–February 9, 1938
Anthon H. Lund	April 5, 1920–March 2, 1921
Anthony W. Ivins	April 5, 1921–October 17, 1934
Ashby Snow	October 17, 1934–April 15, 1936
William L. Walker (3rd VP)	April 22, 1931–(Insufficient stock represented at Stockholders' Meeting; therefore, election invalid.)
R. W. Madsen (3rd VP)	June 14, 1933–April 15, 1936
(2nd VP)	April 15, 1936–April 20, 1938
(1st VP)	April 20, 1938–April 24, 1946
J. Reuben Clark, Jr.	April 20, 1938–April 24, 1946
Harold H. Bennett	May 2, 1946–February 20, 1952
(Exec. VP)	February 20, 1952–April 16, 1958
Stephen L Richards	April 18, 1951–April 16, 1958
Wendell E. Adams	April 16, 1958–May 19, 1970
(VP-Oper.)	May 19, 1970–January 28, 1975
(VP-Pers.)	January 28, 1975–August 1, 1983
Dean R. Williams (VP-Fin.)	May 19, 1970–August 1, 1977
Joseph A. Anderson, Jr. (VP-Merch.)	May 19, 1970–August 1, 1977
(Exec. VP)	August 1, 1977–August 1, 1983
Milo L. Carlston (VP-Oper.)	May 25, 1976–December 31, 1988
W. Keith Mitchell (VP-GMS)	May 25, 1976–August 1, 1977
Keith C. Saunders (VP-Fin.)	August 1, 1977–
(Exec. VP)	April 21, 1986–
John R. Ruppel (VP-Stores)	May 21, 1980–April 13, 1981
(VP-GMM)	April 13, 1981–August 1, 1983
(VP-Sales & Merch.)	August 1, 1983–February 6, 1984
(VP-GMM/Home/Budget/Men's)	February 6, 1984–July 31, 1985
Douglas B. Rogers (VP-GMM)	May 21, 1980–April 13, 1981
(VP-GMM/RTW/Acc.)	February 6, 1984–May 28, 1986

Darrell F. Robinette	October 1, 1981–February 6, 1984
(VP-Stores)	
(VP-Pers.)	February 6, 1984–July 20, 1984
(VP-Strs)	July 20, 1984–
Lowell M. Durham, Jr.	April 1, 1983–August 1, 1983
(VP-Corp Devel.)	
(VP-Pers.)	August 1, 1983–February 6, 1984
(VP-Stores)	February 6, 1984–July 20, 1984
(Exec. VP)	July 20, 1984–January 30, 1985
R. Barry Arnold (GMM)	July 2, 1985–April 21, 1986
(VP-GMM)	April 21, 1986–
Nancy Mortensen (VP-Marketing)	April 21, 1986–

Secretary	Appointment
William Clayton	October 16, 1868–October 5, 1871
Thomas G. Webber	October 5, 1871–October 5, 1876
David O. Calder	October 5, 1876–August 10, 1878
Thomas G. Webber	August 10, 1878–April 5, 1919
C. A. F. Orlob	April 5, 1919–February 15, 1928
Gus P. Backman	April 5, 1926–June 18, 1930
Harold H. Bennett	April 4, 1931–May 2, 1946
J. H. Alleman	May 2, 1946–March 8, 1953
Dean H. Williams	April 21, 1954–August 1, 1977
Keith C. Saunders	August 1, 1977–

Assistant Secretary	Appointment
A. W. Carlson	October 10, 1888–April 20, 1911
C. A. F. Orlob	April 20, 1911–April 5, 1919
Gus P. Backman	April 11, 1923–April 5, 1926
Harold H. Bennett	April 5, 1928–April 4, 1931
Edwin W. Blackhurst	August 17, 1932–April 17, 1940
Dean R. Williams	April 16, 1952–April 21, 1954
Marjorie Beard*	April 18, 1956–September 1, 1983
Ronald L. Culverwell	October 26, 1983–
*First Woman Officer	

175

Treasurer	Appointment
David O. Calder	October 16, 1868–October 5, 1871
Thomas Williams	October 5, 1871–July 7, 1874
John Clark	July 28, 1874–April 1, 1875
Thomas G. Webber	April 1, 1875–October 5, 1876
David O. Calder	October 5, 1876–August 10, 1878
Thomas G. Webber	August 10, 1878–October 5, 1889
A. W. Carlson	October 5, 1889–July 8, 1911
W. S. Romney	August 17, 1911–May 18, 1932
Harold H. Bennett	June 14, 1933–May 2, 1946
Orval W. Adams	May 2, 1946–April 16, 1958
Dean R. Williams	April 16, 1958–August 1, 1977
Keith C. Saunders	August 1, 1977–January 19, 1989
Ronald L. Culverwell	January 19, 1989–

Assistant Treasurer	Appointment
A. W. Carlson	October 10, 1888–October 5, 1889
John H. Burrows	April 20, 1911–May 19, 1926
Harold H. Bennett	December 19, 1928–June 14, 1933

ZCMI CHAIRMAN OF THE BOARD

Name	Appointment
R. W. Madsen	April 24, 1946–May 17, 1948
David O. McKay	April 16, 1958–January 18, 1970
Joseph Fielding Smith	February 27, 1970–July 2, 1972
Harold B. Lee	August 22, 1972–December 26, 1973
Spencer W. Kimball	January 22, 1974–May 27, 1975
N. Eldon Tanner	May 27, 1975–October 15, 1980
Marvin J. Ashton	October 15, 1980–

ZCMI VICE CHAIRMAN OF THE BOARD

Name	Appointment
Stephen L Richards	April 16, 1958–May 19, 1959
J. Reuben Clark, Jr.	April 16, 1958–October 6, 1961
Henry D. Moyle	June 23, 1959–September 1963
Hugh B. Brown	October 24, 1961–February 27, 1970
N. Eldon Tanner	October 29, 1963–May 27, 1975
Harold B. Lee	February 27, 1970–August 22, 1972
Marion G. Romney	August 22, 1972–May 27, 1975
Joseph A. Anderson	February 1, 1985–October 29, 1986
L. Tom Perry	January 21, 1987–

ZCMI GENERAL MANAGERS (Superintendent)

Name	Appointment
H. B. Clawson	March 8, 1869–November 10, 1873
William H. Hooper	November 10, 1873–April 1, 1875
H. B. Clawson	April 13, 1875–October 20, 1876
Horace S. Eldredge	October 20, 1876–January 24, 1881
William Jennings	January 24, 1881–May 31, 1883
Horace S. Eldredge	June 2, 1883–September 6, 1888
Thomas G. Webber	October 10, 1888–April 17, 1919
John F. Bennett	April 15, 1920–January 21, 1931
Gus P. Backman	May 16, 1928–November 13, 1929
William L. Walker	November 13, 1929–June 3, 1933
R. W. Madsen	October 18, 1933–January 29, 1936
Ashby Snow	August 15, 1934–January 29, 1936
R. W. Madsen	January 29, 1936–April 24, 1946
H. H. Bennett	May 2, 1946–February 20, 1952

ZCMI BOARD OF DIRECTORS

Director	Appointment
Brigham Young	October 16, 1868–October 5, 1871
William H. Hooper	October 16, 1868–October 5, 1877
George Q. Cannon	October 16, 1868–January 22, 1874
George A. Smith	October 16, 1868–September 1, 1875
Horace S. Eldredge	October 16, 1868–January 16, 1886
H. W. Lawrence	October 16, 1868–October 5, 1869
William Jennings	October 16, 1868–November 10, 1873
Thomas Taylor	October 5, 1869–October 5, 1871
Hiram B. Clawson	December 1, 1870–October 5, 1877
Theodore McKean	October 5, 1871–October 4, 1873
David Day	October 4, 1873–March 29, 1876
Theodore McKean	November 10, 1873–June 10, 1875
Thomas Jennings	January 22, 1874–May 1, 1874
Albert Carrington	May 1, 1874–October 5, 1875
Christopher Layton	October 5, 1875–October 5, 1876
Aurelius Miner	October 5, 1875–October 5, 1877
David O. Calder	October 5, 1875–October 5, 1877
George Reynolds	October 5, 1876–October 5, 1877
James Jack	October 5, 1876–October 5, 1877
George Q. Cannon	October 5, 1877–April 12, 1901
John Taylor	October 5, 1877–April 5, 1883
Wilford Woodruff	October 5, 1877–October 3, 1879
Brigham Young, Jr.	October 5, 1877–October 5, 1878
John Sharp	October 5, 1877–December 23, 1891
Moses Thatcher	October 5, 1877–October 5, 1888
David O. Calder	October 5, 1878–July 3, 1884
Joseph F. Smith	October 3, 1879–November 19, 1918
S. W. Sears	May 11, 1883–October 5, 1885
George Romney	October 4, 1884–February 1, 1920
John R. Winder	October 5, 1885–March 27, 1910
W. W. Riter	January 16, 1886–April 5, 1886
Heber J. Grant	April 5, 1886–May 14, 1945
Henry Dinwoodey	October 5, 1888–October 1, 1905
P. T. Farnsworth	October 5, 1888–October 2, 1895
John R. Barnes	October 5, 1888–January 21, 1919
W. H. Rowe	October 5, 1888–October 2, 1895
T. W. Jennings	October 5, 1888–April 15, 1891

John Henry Smith	April 15, 1891–October 13, 1911
Francis M. Lyman	April 7, 1892–November 18, 1916
Franklin D. Richards	October 2, 1895–October 15, 1895
L. John Nuttall	October 2, 1895–October 15, 1895
Moses Thatcher	October 2, 1895–April 5, 1897
Wilford Woodruff	October 2, 1895–September 2, 1898
P. T. Farnsworth	October 15, 1895–April 5, 1905
Abraham H. Cannon	October 15, 1895–July 19, 1896
Anthon H. Lund	January 15, 1897–March 2, 1921
William H. McIntyre	April 5, 1897–August 20, 1926
Lorenzo Snow	September 15, 1898–October 10, 1901
Reed Smoot	May 16, 1901–April 5, 1929
Thomas G. Webber	October 17, 1901–August 15, 1920
L. S. Hills	April 5, 1905–July 21, 1915
A. W. Carlson	November 16, 1905–July 8, 1911
Henry M. Dinwoodey	April 5, 1910–June 6, 1937
John F. Bennett	August 17, 1911–February 9, 1938
George Albert Smith	November 16, 1911–April 5, 1933
Edgar S. Hills	August 19, 1915–April 16, 1958
Hyrum M. Smith	April 5, 1917–January 23, 1918
David A. Smith	April 5, 1918–April 5, 1929
Charles W. Nibley	December 19, 1918–December 16, 1931
A. H. Woolley	February 20, 1919–April 5, 1933
W. A. Needham	April 5, 1920–November 9, 1925
Stephen L Richards	April 5, 1921–May 19, 1959
Anthony W. Ivins	April 5, 1921–October 17, 1934
C. A. F. Orlob	April 5, 1926–April 5, 1929
William H. McIntyre, Jr.	November 17, 1926–November 19, 1947
Orval W. Adams	April 5, 1929–May 18, 1968
Henry H. Blood	April 5, 1929–June 19, 1942
Sylvester Q. Cannon	April 5, 1929–May 29, 1943
Richard W. Madsen	April 5, 1932–May 17, 1948
J. Reuben Clark, Jr.	April 5, 1933–October 6, 1961
Ashby Snow	April 5, 1933–April 4, 1936
A. H. Woolley	February 20, 1935–December 26, 1955
Herbert A. Snow	April 4, 1936–November 2, 1957
S. B. Eggertsen	June 6, 1937–April 18, 1951
Harold H. Bennett	March 16, 1938–May 18, 1977
David O. McKay	June 24, 1942–January 18, 1970
LeGrand Richards	April 5, 1944–May 19, 1970

George Albert Smith	May 31, 1945–April 4, 1951
Eric W. Ryberg	February 18, 1948–September 30, 1951
R. W. Madsen, Jr.	June 16, 1948–May 25, 1976
Delbert L. Stapley	April 18, 1951–May 25, 1976
George M. Gadsby	April 18, 1951–March 29, 1960
Alfred B. Smith	April 21, 1954–May 18, 1977
Leo M. Jacobsen	April 18, 1956–June 28, 1966
William F. Edwards	April 16, 1958–April 15, 1959
Ashby Snow	April 16, 1958–April 20, 1960
Henry D. Moyle	June 23, 1959–September, 1963
Leland B. Flint	June 28, 1960–September 22, 1964
Edward M. Naughton	January 24, 1961–May 18, 1977
Hugh B. Brown	October 24, 1961–May 19, 1970
N. Eldon Tanner	October 29, 1963–October 15, 1980
Wendell E. Adams	October 27, 1964–August 1, 1983
Dean R. Williams	October 27, 1964–January 23, 1973
Robert L. Simpson	October 27, 1964–May 27, 1975
E. LaMar Buckner	May 28, 1968–May 27, 1975
Leo M. Jacobsen	August 26, 1969–August 1, 1983
Joseph Fielding Smith	February 27, 1970–July 2, 1972
Harold B. Lee	February 27, 1970–December 26, 1973
Marion G. Romney	August 22, 1972–May 27, 1975
Oakley S. Evans	January 23, 1973–August 1, 1983
Dean R. Williams	May 22, 1973–August 1, 1977
Spencer W. Kimball	January 22, 1974–May 27, 1975
Joseph A. Anderson, Jr.	May 28, 1974–October 29, 1986
L. Tom Perry	May 27, 1975–
Rowland M. Cannon	May 25, 1976–August 1, 1983
Spencer F. Eccles	May 25, 1976–
Patricia F. Madsen	May 25, 1976–
E. Allan Hunter	May 18, 1977–July 18, 1984
Marvin J. Ashton	May 18, 1977–
A. Blaine Huntsman	May 18, 1977–
Dan S. Bushnell	May 16, 1979–
Stephen H. Anderson	April 20, 1981–October 16, 1985
Keith C. Saunders	April 20, 1981–
Milo L. Carlston	April 20, 1981–May 20, 1987
John R. Ruppel	April 20, 1981–July 31, 1985
James S. Jardine	January 22, 1986–
Lela Ence	May 20, 1987–

Richard H. Madsen   May 25, 1988–
R. Barry Arnold   May 23, 1990–
Patricia Holland   July 18, 1990–

ZCMI DIVISIONAL MERCHANDISE MANAGERS

Name	Appointment
Doug Rogers	December 1, 1957–August 8, 1977
Cal Lambert	February 1, 1963–
Richard Childs	February 1, 1963–February 16, 1976
Dean Ence	February 1, 1963–January 31, 1973
Joseph A. Anderson	November 1, 1966–May 19, 1970
Joseph Frodsham	February 1, 1970–
Don MacLean	February 1, 1973–February 1, 1989
Bill Garbett	September 9, 1974–September 22, 1980
Jack Seal	March 1, 1976–July 2, 1985
Terry Memmott	April 7, 1980–August 9, 1982
Richard Burton	April 7, 1980–February 1, 1982
LaNola Cottrell	April 7, 1980–July 1, 1986
John R. Ruppel	April 7, 1980–April 13, 1981
Robert Coppa	August 9, 1982–
Diane Young	February 1, 1982–April 7, 1989
Wayne Andrus	February 1, 1982–
Barry Arnold	February 3, 1983–May 1, 1985
Bob DeWitt	May 1, 1985–
Quincy Stringham	May 4, 1987–
Lorin Hunt	October 3, 1988–
Howard Taylor	April 17, 1989–
Anne Syme	May 21, 1990–

ZCMI STORE MANAGERS

Downtown Store
Salt Lake City, UT   Appointment

Gerald G. Smith	November 1, 1962–January 31, 1975
John R. Ruppel	February 1, 1975–August 1, 1977
W. Keith Mitchell	August 1, 1977–August 1, 1979
Darrell F. Robinette	September 10, 1979–September 10, 1981
G. Robert DeWitt	September 10, 1981–April 26, 1985
Darrell F. Robinette	April 26, 1985–October 7, 1986
V. Thomas Whitesides	October 7, 1986–September 26, 1988
Dell Stokes	September 26, 1988–

Cottonwood Store
Salt Lake City, UT   Appointment
(Opened March 26,
   1962)

Joseph A. Anderson, Jr.	October 1960–November 1, 1966
David S. Hatch	November 1, 1966–May 1, 1985
Douglas B. Rogers	April 26, 1985–February 24, 1986
Heber J. Lloyd	February 24, 1986–

Ogden Store
Ogden, UT   Appointment
(Opened March 6, 1967)

W. Keith Mitchell

	May 1966–February 1, 1970
Donald MacLean	February 1, 1970–February 1, 1973
Durlin Bailey	February 1, 1973–April 13, 1981
Douglas B. Rogers	April 13, 1981–February 6, 1984
Dave Hardman	February 20, 1984–

Valley Fair Store
West Valley, UT   Appointment
(Opened July 27, 1970)

W. Keith Mitchell   February 1, 1970–March 23, 1972
Heber J. Lloyd   March 23, 1972–September 10, 1981
Bill Coles   September 10, 1981–April 19, 1986
Dell Stokes   April 19, 1986–September 26, 1988
V. Thomas Whitesides   September 26, 1988–

University Store
Provo, UT   Appointment
(Opened November 24,
    1972)

W. Keith Mitchell   March 23, 1972–April 1974
Darrell F. Robinette   April 1974–September 10, 1979
G. Robert DeWitt   September 10, 1979–September 10, 1981
Heber J. Lloyd   September 10, 1981–February 24, 1986
Ron Farley   February 24, 1986–

Cache Valley Store
Logan, UT   Appointment
(Opened July 28, 1976)

Richard H. Child   January 27, 1976–February 1, 1979
David Hardman   February 1, 1979–February 6, 1984
Rod Pack   February 20, 1984–

Layton Hills Store
Layton, UT   Appointment
(Opened April 24, 1980)

V. Thomas Whitesides   February 1, 1980–October 7, 1986
David Haight   October 7, 1986–

Pine Ridge Store
<u>Pocatello, ID</u>   <u>Appointment</u>
(Opened July 29, 1981)

Ron Farley   April 22, 1981–March 1, 1986
Patricia Peyton   March 1, 1986–June 5, 1989
Don Bushman   June 5, 1989–

Grand Teton Store
<u>Idaho Falls, ID</u>   <u>Appointment</u>
(Opened July 31, 1984)

Erven Thurman   February 20, 1984–

South Towne Store
<u>Sandy, UT</u>   <u>Appointment</u>
(Opened July 28, 1986)

Ken Kraudy   May 28, 1986–

Red Cliffs/St. George
   Store
<u>St. George, UT</u>   <u>Appointment</u>
(Opened June 1, 1987 &
   August 1, 1990)

John Stanford   May 4, 1987–

ZCMI II STORE MANAGERS

Fashion Place Store
Murray, UT   Appointment
(Opened August 4,
   1988)

Bruce Larson   February 1, 1988–May 21, 1990
Roland Elison   May 21, 1990–

Foothill Store
Salt Lake City, UT   Appointment
(Opened August 4,
   1988)

Bruce Larson   February 1, 1988–May 21, 1990
Hiru Jorgensen   May 21, 1990–December 31, 1990
Steve Ericksson   December 31, 1990–

Tri City Store
Mesa, Arizona   Appointment
(Opened March 1, 1990)

Anne Syme   September 14, 1989–May 21, 1990
Allison Moon   May 21, 1990–August 1, 1990
Jackie Anderson   August 1, 1990–

East Bay Store
Provo, UT   Appointment
(Opened March 1, 1990)

Bruce Larson   September 14, 1989–May 21, 1990
Vic Walsh   May 21, 1990–

Scottsdale Pavilions
   Store
Scottsdale, AZ   Appointment
(Opened Sept. 7, 1990)

Allison Moon   August 1, 1990–October 1, 1990
B. J. Spohn   October 1, 1990–

Village Fair North Store
Phoenix, AZ

                       Appointment
(Opened Nov. 15, 1990)

Allison Moon   October 1, 1990–December 31, 1990
Kristin Adams   Dec. 31, 1990–

Superstition Springs
   Store
Mesa, AZ   Appointment
(Opened Feb. 6, 1990)

Allison Moon   December 31, 1990–

Charleston Commons
Las Vegas, NV   Appointment
(Opened Feb. 13, 1990)

Hiru Jorgensen   December 31, 1990–

ZCMI MANAGEMENT 1990

Richard Madsen	President/C.E.O.
Keith Saunders	Executive Vice President
Barry Arnold	Vice President, G.M.M.
Nancy Mortensen	Vice President, Marketing Services
Darrell Robinette	Vice President, Stores
Bill Coles	Executive Assistant to the President
Ron Culverwell	Corporate Treasurer
Brent Whipple	Comptroller
Reese Merrill	Corporate Personnel Manager
Earl Russell	Corporate Credit Manager
Jack Seal	Merchandise Director
Howard Taylor	D.M.M., Ready to Wear
Loren Hunt	D.M.M., Juniors' and Children's Wear
Robert Coppa	D.M.M., Fashion Accessories
Joe Frodsham	D.M.M., Men's Wear
Quincy Stringham	D.M.M., Smallwares
Cal Lambert	D.M.M., Home Furnishings
Bob DeWitt	D.M.M., Decorative Home
Wayne Andrus	D.M.M., Cost and Lease
Anne Syme	D.M.M., ZCMI II
Dell Stokes	Store Manager, Downtown
Heber Lloyd	Store Manager, Cottonwood
Dave Hardman	Store Manager, Ogden
Tom Whitesides	Store Manager, Valley Fair
Ron Farley	Store Manager, University Mall
Rod Pack	Store Manager, Cache Valley
David Haight	Store Manager, Layton Hills
Don Bushman	Store Manager, Pine Ridge
Erven Thurman	Store Manager, Grand Teton
Ken Kraudy	Store Manager, South Towne
John Stanford	Store Manager, St. George/Red Cliffs
Bruce Larsen	Director of ZCMI II Stores
Brent Baker	Director of Advertising
Mike Stevens	Director of Visual Merchandising
Fred Parkin	Manager of Store Planning
Dave Hill	Manager of Systems
Greg Bowden	Internal Auditor
Vern Morgan	Training Director

Dick Monson	Marketing Analyst
Glenn Hogge	Merchandise Comptroller
Susan Collins	Fashion Director
Golden Poor	Service Center Manager
Dale Magleby	Manager of Marking and Receiving
Dale Pascoe	Manager of Security
Ronn Jones	Assistant Advertising Director
Fay Shifflett	Director of Special Events

APPENDIX C

HISTORIC QUOTATIONS

1. Brigham Young

It is not for the purpose of making money that Zion's Co-operative Mercantile Institution is to be established. A higher object than this prompts its organization. A union of interests is sought to be attained. The Latter-day Saints are acting in utter disregard of the principles of self-preservation. They are encouraging the growth of evils in their own midst which they condemned as the worst features of the systems from which they have gathered. Large profits are being concentrated in comparatively few hands, instead of being generally distributed among the people. As a consequence, the community is being rapidly divided into classes and the hateful and unhappy distinctions which the possession and lack of wealth give rise to are becoming painfully apparent. . . . In the absence of the necessary faith to enter upon a more perfect order revealed by the Lord unto the Church, this is felt to be the best means of drawing us together and making us one.

2. ZCMI *Advocate,* Message from Management

A good businessman is never satisfied with superficial ideas in regard to that which he is engaged — he considers ignorance inexcusable if he has had an opportunity to learn;

The businessman is no idler, he enjoys work, realizing that "the hand of the diligent maketh rich";

The true businessman does not want for acknowledgement, for patronage, for trade — he creates it;

The true businessman does not waste his strength on side issues; he is not speculative in that sense, there is concentration about him, it is his atmosphere, he is a man of purpose;

A true businessman is prudent, economical thrifty; waste is his abhorrence, trifles are to him unknown, small savings makes large havings;

A true businessman is orderly—everything in its place, and there is a place for everything; books, papers, accounts, goods are all straight, understandable, correct.

A true businessman is also honest in all his transactions; integrity, truth, honor are watchwords;

A true businessman is a man of his word, he is truthful, he never misrepresents; he meets his obligations promptly; he is always on time, punctuality rules his movements.

The true businessman is a man of God. Some object to this, and consider religion and business are aliens and strangers to each other, some consider them absolute enemies, yet are they husband and wife.

3. *Deseret News,* March 3, 1876

It [ZCMI] is a three story building, with basement extending under the whole of the structure, and the iron front, designed by Folsom and Taylor, is very handsome, making it a splendid appearance . . . the basement will be used for the storage of the various classes of heavy goods, and at the rear . . . are the engine and boiler, used for hoisting and lowering the elevator . . . and heating the huge building by means of pipes and steam. Nine hundred thousand bricks were used in the construction of the building. No less than 16,897 square feet of tin was used on the roof. Three thousand feet of lumber was used in the building. The basement is 11 feet in the clear, the first floor is 17 feet in the clear, the second 15 feet and third 12 feet. The first floor would contain the retail dry goods and notions department; the wholesale and retail boot and shoe, leather and findings department; and the retail grocery and hardware department. Also at the back were the offices of the establishment and the area for the receiving and delivery of goods. The second floor contained the wholesale dry goods, notions and carpets department, the wholesale grocery and hardware business, and the opening and marking room. The third floor was devoted to hollow and willow ware and the packing room.

4. Letter from Brigham Young, March 28, 1875, to Elder Alma L. Smith, Sandwich Islands

Dear Brother:

Zion's Co-operative Mercantile Institution is now moving into its new store. A short description of which will probably be of interest to yourself and the Elders from home, as it has been built entirely under my personal direction and supervision. Exactly eleven months ago the ground was broken for this mammoth building and the work of excavating the cellar commenced. The edifice is peculiar in its construction all the light being received from the front and top, there are no windows in all the vast extent of its side walls which are 318 feet long. Its frontage is 53 feet and it is four stories, including the cellar, in height. Its front, which is on East Temple Street, is massive and chaste, being composed of iron and plate glass. The light is abundant, and the ventilation excellent, the cellar of the building will be used for the storage of heavy goods, the first or ground floor will be devoted to the retail trade, the next floor above will be occupied by the wholesale department and the top floor will be used as a warehouse for the lighter classes of goods. The interior is

tastefully though plainly fitted up and from the general stair-
case presents a grand "couf d'oil" [sic] which impresses the
mind with the vastness of the building and its extraordinary
adaptability to the doing of a heavy business with as little
expense and unnecessary handling of goods as possible.

I remain, Your Brother in the Gospel covenant,
Brigham Young

5. ZCMI Building Description, *Journal History*
June 25, 1875

The foundation of the ZCMI new building is being made
of the most substantial character. At each of the four corners
is an excavation six feet deep and four feet by six feet in
extent, and filled with strong concrete and rock, forming a
firm, solid mass. Besides these there are five dig-outs, five
feet deep below the footing, prepared and filled similarly to
corner excavations. Upon these, as well as the ground between, the foundation will rest. The foundation wall will have
a width of two feet six inches at the bottom, tapering to two
feet at the top of the basement.

All around the inside of the wall, at distances of only twelve
feet apart, will be eighteen inch square buttresses, in each
of which will be two thimbles for ventilation registers, one
row about two feet above the footing and the upper one
about fifteen inches below the ceiling, to carry away everything in the shape of foul air, the flumes running clear to the
roof.

August 3, 1875

The ZCMI new building continues to go up rapidly, Mr.
Henry Grow and his corps of hands have nearly finished the
laying of the joists of the first floor, all of the timbers of which,
including the huge supports, are of excellent Utah red pine,
which for strength and durability can scarcely be excelled.

December 15, 1875

At present the cellar is being made, by putting down two
by six inch scantling a foot apart, and filling in all over between them with concrete, made with lime and gravel, the
job taking probably about fifteen hundred loads of material.
Upon this solid accummulation will be placed a double floor
of red pine lumber.

March 3, 1876

It is a three story building, with basement extending under
the whole of the structure, and the iron front, designed by
Folsom and Taylor, is very handsome, making a splendid
appearance. In constructing the basement, which is eleven
feet high in the clear, 219 cords of rock was used. The floor
of this part is of the most solid description, being formed in
the first place by filling from the ground to the level of the
upper edge of the joists with concrete, and over this hard
material is laid two courses of flooring. The brick of which
the walls are composed was manufactured by Bountiful Cooperative Institution, no less than 900,000 of the article being
used in their construction, and had they been the ordinary
fixed brick, instead of larger, it would have taken one third
more.

On the roof there is no less than 16,897 square feet of tin,
placed there by Mitchell and James.

Necessarily a large amount of lumber has been used in the
construction, the approximation being about 575,000 feet,
most of which, especially the heavier timbers, is good, sound,
durable red pine. Each floor is supported by rows of pillars
or columns, 48 on each, aggregating 192, those above the
basement being turned.

The first floor is 17 feet in the clear, the second 15 feet and
the third 12 feet.

A distinguishing feature, of the building is being lighted from the roof, as previously stated. The horizontal measurement across the skylights is 10 feet, the opening down the middle of the third floor 10 feet also, and that on the second floor 12 feet, this arrangement admitting a flood of light to the whole interior. Before the structure was so far advanced some expressed doubts as to the sufficiency of the light by this means, but the result attained has dispelled all ideas of that kind, and it is as well if not better lighted than any building of magnitude in the Territory. The openings in the upper floors are bridged over at intervals, to admit of passing from one side to another, and those bridges, as well as the whole sides of the openings, are surrounded by a suitable railing, in the form of flat bannisters.

President Young was that originator, and not only was the building got up on his design, but he has personally supervised the construction of every part, which is alone a warrant of substantiality for everything about the entire structure, he being, on principle opposed to anything being made a part of a building that is of a filmsy or unenduring character, and the whole result is a monument of the keen sensibility of his mind to the general fitness of things.

6. Letter from R. W. Madsen to employees, September 1, 1938

A Personal Letter to Every Employee:

For any firm to succeed there must exist two essential factors: SERVICE AND PROFIT. If either one is lacking or absent, the store will be short lived.

Reasonable PROFIT is absolutely essential to pay employees a fair wage, to give investors in the company a just return for the money they have invested, and to give the public efficient service.

Service is efficiency, courtesy, thoroughness and a desirability to be helpful to the customer and store. Service is the thing that makes people think favorably or unfavorably about you and your firm. Have you ever asked yourself, "What is it that people whom I have waited on, will remember and like about me?" It can in one sense be known as GOOD WILL. . . .

For a firm or an individual to be more than ordinary, it or he must *do* more than the ordinary. To excel your competitor as a store or an individual you must be willing to do more than your competitor.

You must do the thing necessary in the unusual way, and in the courteous way. Successful leaders of men in successful companies, never master obstacles by indifference, lack of interest or unwillingness. They constantly prepare themselves, burn the midnight oil and do more than is asked of them. They always try to do the right thing at the right time. Their efforts are repaid by promotion and personal pride. "By thy work thou shalt be known."

Should not every employee give his entire time, thoughts and service to his company during working hours? Should he be permitted to run out of the store for an hour or more at a time on personal business or social calls? You can readily see the unfairness of such a condition. Personal matters should be done before or after working hours, or during lunch hour so that all worries of an outside nature can be abolished. Be sold on your job, your firm and your boss. Never let it be called to your attention that you are out of line. Keep in tune with progress, industry, service and the unfaltering determination to fill the unforgiving minute with sixty seconds worth of distance run.

Fall is here and our business will naturally swell. However, our increase will be more than normal, if each of us lifts his feet so that there will be no dragging whatsoever. It is a better feeling to be on the construction crew than on the wrecking gang. Give a 100 percent honest effort and attendance to making your company a huge success. Your efforts have not gone by unnoticed and from my heart, I tell you, I personally appreciate every good turn you do for this splendid organization. Let's continue to clasp hands and to push forward. As a firm, as a manager, as an employee let's not only be willing, but let's do more than any of our competitors in our respected field to bring an unusual mutual success to our store, and pride of accomplishment to us all.

Yours and mine, for a greater fall business

R. W. Madsen

INDEX

Adams, Wendell, 99, 126
Allred, John, 53
Amos Parrish Fashion Office, 102
Anderson, Joseph, 113, 126, 141, 147–149
Anderson, Stephen, 149
"Apostolic Circular," 29–30
"Approval business," 52–53
Arnold, R. Barry, 155
Ashton, Marvin J., 148–49, 156, 164–65
Auto Centers, 138

Baird, Steven, 131–34
Barnes, Claude, 65–66
Barnes, John R., 61
Barnum, P.T., 2
Barter trade, 53
Beard, Marjorie, 100
Bennett, Harold H.: tells story of retiree's mother, 6–7; directs ZCMI's cooperation with war effort, 92–93; becomes general manager, 98–99; becomes ZCMI president, 109–10; speaks at opening of Cottonwood Mall store, 113–14; praises David O. McKay's breadth of vision, 120; retirement of, 122–24
Bennett, John F., 64–67, 98
Bogardus, James, 131

Book reviews, 104
Bridal services, 104
Brigham City, Utah, cooperative in, 31
Budget Store, decision to discontinue, 156, 161
Bushnell, Dan, 149
Bywater, Annie, 68–69, 76

Calder, David O., 17, 33
Cannon, George Q., 8, 13–14, 15–17, 33, 44–45, 51
Carlston, Milo, 125, 126, 139, 148
Carrington, Albert, 13
Cast iron, use of, in nineteenth-century buildings, 131
Centennial celebration of ZCMI, 120–22
Centralization of operations, 96, 127–30, 139
Child laborers, 68–69
Church of Jesus Christ of Latter-day Saints, The: connection of ZCMI with, 4, 30, 32–33; cooperatives promoted by, 9–10, 28–30; declining role of, in ZCMI, 56–57, 84; opposes unionization, 89–90
Clark, J. Reuben, 109–10
Clawson, Hiram B., 8, 20, 23, 33

Clayton, William, 8, 16, 17, 22, 23

Clothing factory of ZCMI, 44, 76; closing of, 109

Condie, George, 100

Cooperatives: protecting economic life of Saints, 9–10; early proponents of, 13–14; Brigham Young joins campaign for, 14; Rochdale system of, 14, 30; established throughout territory, 15–16, 23, 28; local, became threat to parent store, 20; lauded as "great leveler," 28–29; promoted in "Apostolic Circular," 29–30; in Brigham City, Utah, 31; failure of, in 1890s, 52; sale of remaining, in 1930s, 105–6

"Commitment to Excellence" program, 151–52

Cottonwood Mall store, 113–14

Credit buying, 146–47, 153

Customer Service Advisory Board, 153

Customer services, 104–5; increased emphasis on, 151–53

Davis, Carol, 141

Depression, effect of, on ZCMI, 85–87

Deseret Tanning and Manufacturing Association, 40–41

Deseret Weekly News, 13, 21–22, 34

Dun and Company, 38

Durham, Lowell M., Jr.: becomes vice president of stores, 148; establishes "Commitment to Excellence" program, 151–52; emphasizes customer service with "Extras Make Excellence," 152–53; serves as president of ZCMI, 153–57; confidence of, in employees, 154; major policy changes effected by, 161; resignation of, 165

Eagle Emporium, 23

Eccles, Spencer, 149, 157

Edmunds-Tucker Bill, 43

Eldredge, Horace S., 16, 17, 20, 33–34, 48

Emerson, Ralph Waldo, 38

Employee programs and issues, 70–73, 100–102, 139–41

Ennis, Dorothy, 99

Erickson, Charles E., 63

Evans, Oakley S., 124–27; stresses support for community, 127; announces progress on new downtown store, 134; aggressive merchandising strategy of, 137; focus of, on fashion leadership, 142

Expansion: new era of, 114–15; capital for, 115; into Ogden, 118–19; continuing plan of, 119–20, 122, 149, 163; growth in sales following, 122, 137

"Extras Make Excellence" program, 152–53

Facade, historic, restoration of, 130–34
Fashion: increasing concern with, 102–4, 142–44; upscale, of ZCMI II stores, 162–63
Fashion shows, 102, 104, 143–44
Five-Year Strategic Plan, 163–64
Freed, Christie, 130

Gates Rubber, 138
Gentiles: breach between Mormons and, 10; boycott against firms of, 11–12; businesses of, close, 12
Gift wrap, free, 152
Gorder, Joyce, 143–44
Grant, Heber J., 43, 58, 59–61, 64–65, 95–96
Grow, Henry, 192

Halton, Henry, 83
Home manufacturing, 13, 25–26, 40; decline of, 50–51
Hooper, William H., 13, 16, 17, 33; as president of ZCMI, 39–40, 43
Hunter, Allan, 149

"Indian days," 53
Inflation, skyrocketing, 146
Inventory: LIFO calculation of, 146; tracking, by store, 161

Jennings, William, 8, 17, 20, 23, 46
Joseph Magnin, 135

Kelly, John, 91
Kimball, J. Golden, 39
King, Corrine, 141–42

Labor unions, 89–91
Lawrence, Henry W., 8, 17
Layton, Christopher, 33
Leased departments, 137–38
Lee, Harold B., 131
LIFO calculation of inventory, 146
Logan, Utah, ZCMI store, 144
Logo of ZCMI, 19–20
Lumber, select, used for ZCMI, 6–7
Lund, Anthon H., 65

Mademoiselle magazine, 103
Madsen, Francis Armstrong, 166
Madsen, Patricia H., 149, 165
Madsen, Richard H., 165–68
Madsen, Richard W., 95–98, 149, 165, 194–96
Madsen, Richard W., Jr., 165
Marti, Rosina, 72–73
Maughan, Bishop, 32
McKay, David O., 113–14, 120
Metals Manufacturing Company, 132
Meyer, Fred, 67
Midgley and Evans, 20
Miner, Aurelia, 33
Mission Statement, 161–62
Mitchell, Keith, 125–26, 138–39
Modernization efforts, 74–75
Mortensen, Nancy, 127, 154–55
Mutual Aid Society, 70, 101–2

Naisbett, Henry W., 8, 23
National Recovery
    Administration, 86–87
National Retail Merchants
    Association, 99
Nelson, Harry, 99
Nelson, Ron, 144

Officers and directors of
    ZCMI, 173–88
Ogden, Utah: ZCMI opens
    branch store in, 36–37; sale
    of branch store in, 79; ZCMI
    returns to, 118–19
Oil prices, leap in, 145–46

Parkinson, Lillian, 6–7
Patriotic concerns of ZCMI,
    73–74, 92–94
Perry, D.H., 37
Perry, L. Tom, 149
Phillips, Rueul, 105–6
Price matching, 152, 162

Railroad, anticipated problems
    of, 9
Rampton, Calvin L., 129
Recession, 146–47
Reed, George, 68
Retiree's mother tells story at
    party, 6–7
Return policy, 152
Reynolds, George, 33, 65
Richards, Daniel B., 73
Richards, LeGrand, 113
Rochdale system of
    cooperation, 14, 30
Romney, George, 61
Rowe, William H., 41, 51–52
Rumel Pattern Shop, 132

Ruppel, John, 126, 136, 148

Saddler and Teasdale, 20
Sales, growth in, following
    expansion, 122, 137
Sales experiences, exceptional,
    141–42
Santa Claus, helicopter arrival
    of, 104
Saunders, Keith, 126, 146, 148,
    149, 155
Saville, James Maurice, 68
Seare, William T., 67
Sears, Septimus, 51
Service center, 127–30
Sharp, John, 13, 45
Shoe department, leased, 137–
    38
Shoe factory, 40–41, 76
Skousen, Cleon, 106
Sloan, William, 41
Smith, Alma L., 191
Smith, George A., 16, 17, 40
Smith, Joseph F., 59
Smoot, Abraham O., 15
Snow, Ashby, 96
Snow, Erastus, 25
Snow, L.C., 77
Snow, Lorenzo, 59
South Towne store, 160–61
Springer, Besse, 104
Standard Furniture, 95–96
State Brass Foundry, 132
Stenhouse, T.B.H., 62
Stock of ZCMI: first issues of,
    17, 19; early dividends on,
    26; devaluation of, 91–92;
    revaluing of, 109; trends of,
    144–45; chart showing
    dividends paid on, 169–72

Stoves, men buy, from Gentile store, 32
Strong, R.J., 77

Tanner, Nathan Eldon, 124
Taylor, John, 43–48
Teen fashion board, 144
Thomson, Andy, 142
Truman, Harry S, 106
Turner, Marjorie, 104
Turnover of stock, 79–80

"Underground," polygamous Church leaders go, 43
Unemployment, 86
Union Vedette, 11–12
Unionization, 89–91
University Mall store, 122, 123
Utah: gains statehood, 55; increased urbanization of, 57–58; economic depression in, 80–82

Visual Merchandising's International Display Competition, 144

Wages: legislation concerning, 87–88; postwar, 100–101; scale of, upgraded, 139
Wagner Act, 90
Walker, William L., 82–83, 91, 96
Webber, Thomas G., 48, 51, 61–64
Wedding Gift Registry, 104, 152–53
Weisfeld Jewelers, 135
Wells, Daniel H., 8, 13

Western Steel and Christiansen Bros., 134
Wholesale division of ZCMI, 90, 107–8, 110
Williams, Dean R., 126
Window displays, prize-winning, 144
Wohl Shoe Company, 137–38
Woodmansee, Joseph, 8
Woodruff, Asahel H., 63
Woodruff, Wilford, 8, 15, 48, 59
Woolley, Edwin D., 13
World War II, 92–95

Young, Brigham: dedicates first ZCMI store to Lord, 8; is ZCMI's first customer, 9; cooperative system envisioned by, 9–10; urges Mormons to become merchants, 11, 13; advises boycott of Gentile firms, 12; encourages home manufacturing, 13; joins campaign for cooperative buying, 14–15; encourages all Saints to invest in co-ops, 16; subscribes to ZCMI stock, 17; becomes ZCMI's first president, 17; discusses fair price standards, 17, 22; asks local co-ops to join ZCMI, 20–21; expresses need for retail store, 24; decries division among retailers, 25; loans ZCMI large sum of money, 33; death of, 38–39; smashes inferior mirror with cane,